DNA

for
NATIVE AMERICAN
GENEALOGY

DNA

for

NATIVE AMERICAN
GENEALOGY

Roberta Estes

Genealogical Publishing Co., Inc.

Published by Genealogical Publishing Company
Baltimore, Maryland
2021

ISBN 9780806321189

Front cover:
Rabbit Head—Hidatsa: Library of Congress,
Prints and Photographs Division, Edward S. Curtis Collection
[LC-USZ62-96191]

At the Water's Edge—Arikara: Library of Congress,
Prints and Photographs Division, Edward S. Curtis Collection
[LC-USZ62-107915]

Apache Still Life: Library of Congress,
Prints and Photographs Division, Edward S. Curtis Collection
[LC-USZ62-130198]

Sedona Native American Rock Art,
David Sunfellow

Back cover:
At the Water's Edge—Piegan: Library of Congress,
Prints and Photographs Division, Edward S. Curtis Collection
[LC-USZ62-101262]

Quilt by Roberta Estes

Cover Design by Kate Boyer

This book is dedicated to the Ancestors.
I am honored to bring their story to life.

CONTENTS

PART 3: DNA Testing Vendors and Autosomal Tools

PART 4: Mitochondrial DNA – Ancient and Modern

PART 6: YOUR ROADMAP AND CHECKLIST

ACKNOWLEDGMENTS

I would like to thank the millions of people who have tested their DNA. Their investment helps them find their ancestors, but it also helps us find ours through intersections and interaction with others. We are all interconnected.

I would like to thank Bennett Greenspan and Max Blankfeld, visionary pioneers who founded FamilyTreeDNA in 2000, following Bennett's dream as a genealogist to use Y DNA to confirm his family ancestral links. Thanks to Bennett and two decades of investment in scientific research and the genealogy community, we can find and confirm our ancestors too.

I would like to thank the National Geographic Society, which saw the potential of connecting the world and launched the Genographic Project in April 2005. Offering testers the option of allowing anonymous academic research on their samples has provided indispensable geographic, tribal, language, and haplogroup information for this book.

I would like to thank my colleagues Dr. Miguel Vilar, Genographic Project Lead Scientist; Dr. Paul Maier, Population Geneticist at FamilyTreeDNA; and Goran Runfeldt, Head of Research and Development at FamilyTreeDNA. Advances in the Y DNA tree and the Million Mito Project are rewriting the history of humanity.

I would like to thank the volunteer project administrators who founded and administer projects at FamilyTreeDNA. Their passion and dedication facilitate collaboration by encouraging testers to join projects of interest and relevance to their family research.

I would like to thank the four major testing companies: FamilyTreeDNA, which provides autosomal, mitochondrial, and Y DNA tests; and MyHeritage, Ancestry, and 23andMe, which provide autosomal testing to the genealogical community. Each company provides unique tools that assist genealogists in their never-ending quest for every possible tidbit that can be excavated about our ancestors. I have utilized screenshots of my own test results at each vendor.

I would like to thank my mother, who was an early DNA tester, then encouraged me to use genetics to find people's ancestors and tell their stories, and my stepfather, who assured me that I could do anything.

I would like to thank my husband, Jim, who has faithfully supported my genealogy addiction as I chase those elusive ancestors, and who has made dinner hundreds of times so that I could write undisturbed.

Thank you for reading this book.

INTRODUCTION

Millions of people have family stories involving Native American, First Nations, or indigenous American heritage. Your family may be one of them. Those much-cherished legends often encourage people to take DNA tests to shed light on the stories and discover the identity of Native American ancestors. If this describes you, you're far from alone. In fact, you're in good company.

It's important to first understand the history of Native Americans in the Americas, the circumstances that may have allowed your Native ancestors to become lost in time. My goal is to help you locate these ancestors.

In this book I've included step-by-step instructions for how to use the different types of DNA testing available at the four major DNA testing companies to further your genealogy and confirm or identify Native American ancestors.

What can you expect when you identify that ancestor? Can you become a member of a tribe? Just how do you identify which of your ancestral lines has Native American ancestors? What if your own DNA doesn't show Native heritage? Are you sunk? How can you utilize the DNA of family members? I address all these questions and more.

I start by discussing how DNA works, how much of your Native ancestor's DNA you might expect to inherit, and how to find that DNA.

Testing companies FamilyTreeDNA, MyHeritage, Ancestry, and 23andMe, as well as popular third-party tools like DNAPainter, all offer unique tools for genealogists. You will learn how to utilize each of these tools, separately and together, leveraging every aspect of DNA testing.

I don't stop there, however. I also focus on which haplogroups are found in specific tribes. You'll find ancient DNA information, compiled by haplogroup and mapped. Is your Native American ancestor's haplogroup found in burials? If so, where and what can it tell you about your own ancestor?

DNA testing may be just the tool you need to reveal your ancestors, the goal of every genealogist.

PART 1

SEEKING NATIVE ANCESTORS

Who Are Indigenous People?

Many people living throughout North, Central, and South America either consider themselves to be indigenous Americans or have indigenous ancestors. The word "indigenous" used in this context means people who lived in the Americas pre-contact/colonization by European (or other) cultures, including Africans imported as part of the slave trade.

Today, Native descendants are generally (but not always) mixed. When we combine traditional genealogy research with genetic testing, we get the tools we need to unravel past relationships in order to both identify and understand our ancestors.

People whose Native heritage is not mixed are not generally the people seeking their Native roots through either DNA testing or genealogy. They already know they are Native and probably belong to a tribe. Their DNA tests, in addition to matching family members, help other mixed people identify their Native ancestors and, along with them, that missing piece of their family history.

In Canada the more than 600 indigenous tribes south of the Arctic Circle are referred to collectively as the First Nations or First Nations People. Indigenous people in the Arctic or pan-Arctic area are referred to as Inuit, formerly known as Eskimo, which is now considered an offensive term. Even the correct usage of the term indigenous is sometimes debated.

The term Métis refers to Canadian communities or descendants of mixed indigenous and (generally) European heritage. The Métis may or may not be organized. Tribes or First Nations People may be connected by language, geography, culture, and/or history.

In the United States, indigenous people were historically referred to as Indians, but that term has somewhat fallen out of favor and is considered offensive by some, but not by all. Some Native, indigenous, or aboriginal people call themselves Indians, but others do not. Today, people of indigenous descent are generally referred to as Native Americans, American Indians, or indigenous Americans.

If you're thinking this is a bit messy and maybe slightly awkward, you'd be right!

The indigenous people of Hawaii are closely related to the indigenous people of the Pacific Islands, Polynesia, Australia, and New Zealand.[1]

Indigenous people in the Caribbean fall within the Caribbean archipelago, having arrived to settle those islands from Central and South America.

Texas and the American Southwest were settled, in part, by indigenous people with roots deep in present-day Mexico.

The Diné-speaking Athabascan[2] people, specifically the Navajo and related tribes, migrated from Northwest Canada and present-day Alaska to present-day Arizona and New Mexico, extending into southeastern Utah roughly 600 years ago, a journey still reflected in their legends.[3]

In Canada and the United States, respectively, members of tribes may have rights based on treaty status.[4] Federally recognized tribes in the United States have a government-to-government relationship with specific obligations and responsibilities set forth for both parties, although historically the United States government has breached most or all of the more than 500 treaties to which they were a party.[5]

Indigenous peoples found in the Caribbean and West Indies are sometimes, within the islands, referred to as ethnic groups. They are genetically connected to South America, with the exception of some indigenous people who were transported as slaves from the eastern seaboard of the United States in colonial times, during and following the Tuscarora War (1711–1715).[6] Conversely, enslaved people were transported from the Caribbean to the American Colonies as well.

People born in the Caribbean or with ancestors from the islands often discover via DNA testing that they have indigenous ancestors and may be connected to peoples in either North or South America.

While the United States and Canada designate tribes as both legal and social entities, Mexico does not. Mexico defines itself in its constitution as a "pluricultural nation," in recognition of the various ethnic groups that represent cultures today.[7] Having said that, some people in Mexico and Mesoamerica[8] can and do associate themselves with the Maya or Inca people, for example, or with smaller regional groups.

---

[1] https://en.wikipedia.org/wiki/Pacific_Islander
[2] https://en.wikipedia.org/wiki/Athabaskan_languages
[3] Pritzker, Barry M. *A Native American Encyclopedia: History, Culture, and Peoples.* Oxford: Oxford University Press, 2000
[4] https://www.bia.gov/frequently-asked-questions; https://en.wikipedia.org/wiki/List_of_United_States_treaties
[5] https://en.wikipedia.org/wiki/List_of_United_States_treaties
[6] https://en.wikipedia.org/wiki/Tuscarora_War
[7] https://en.wikipedia.org/wiki/Indigenous_peoples_of_Mexico#cite_note-CDI-3
[8] https://en.wikipedia.org/wiki/Mesoamerica

In 2015, according to the National Commission for the Development of Indigenous People, more than 25 million people, or 21% of the Mexican population, self-identify as being members of different indigenous ethnic groups based on language alone. People speaking only Spanish were excluded, so the total of residents who have indigenous ancestors would be much higher. Genealogists familiar with the concept of "tribes" might recognize these groups as the names of historical pre-colonization indigenous people today, such as the Maya, the Aztec, and 15 other groups of indigenous peoples, generally connected by language.[9]

Interestingly, in 2011 the paper "Large scale mitochondrial sequencing in Mexican Americans suggests a reappraisal of Native American origins"[10] included information indicating that 85–90% of Mexican American individuals carry indigenous mitochondrial DNA, inherited directly from their mother's mother's mother's direct matrilineal line, while their autosomal DNA reflected only 30–46% indigenous ancestry.

This clearly shows a scientific pattern referred to as "directional mating," where one population selectively mates with another population. Of course, in the case of Mexico and Mesoamerica, selective mating was the result of Spanish or European men having children with Native women, in part because there were few European women in the "New World." Add to that the institution of slavery.

Native females passed their indigenous mitochondrial DNA to both sexes of their children, but only their daughters passed it through all female lines to be found in descendants of both sexes in the generations living today.

Clearly, DNA testing is one avenue through which we can identify indigenous ancestors, even if their identity has been lost to our family history.

The indigenous peoples of Mexico, the United States bordering Mexico, and Mesoamerica cannot be cleanly separated by the political boundaries of countries today. People migrate and boundaries are fluid.

The settlement of the Americas progressed over time from the furthest Northwest Alaskan peninsula to the southern tip of South America. Successive waves of people lived in and crossed over the now-submerged passageway of Beringia[11] connecting the Chukotka Peninsula in Siberia with the Seward Peninsula in present-day Alaska.

Scientists have debated for years whether the people who became indigenous Americans arrived in one or multiple successive waves. Another area of continuing research focuses on whether a coastal migration route existed in addition to the Beringian model. There is

---

[9] https://en.wikipedia.org/wiki/Indigenous_peoples_of_Mexico
[10] https://bmcevolbiol.biomedcentral.com/track/pdf/10.1186/1471-2148-11-293.pdf
[11] https://en.wikipedia.org/wiki/Beringia

also debate, but no proof yet, that at some point Polynesians may have reached the shores of South America and integrated into the local culture.

Research into the peopling of the Americas continues today at a rapid clip, aided by successful genetic sequencing in the emerging field of ancient DNA.[12]

Due to cultural and religious beliefs and concerns, some tribes in the United States resist or discourage DNA testing of tribal members, as well as forbid the testing of the remains of people they consider to be their ancestors. DNA testing remains controversial, although some tribes have formed alliances with select, trusted researchers.

The respectful treatment of the remains according to the culture and involvement of tribal members is of paramount importance in DNA testing. NAGPRA, the United States Native American Graves Protection and Repatriation Act[13] of 1990, seeks to remedy earlier unlawful excavations, desecration, and exploitation of indigenous graves and cultural objects—providing an avenue for repatriation of objects currently in the custody of museums and other government organizations and preventing current and future abuses.[14]

As this relates to genetic genealogy, the effect is that there are fewer ancient Native samples available for study in the United States, and tribal members are sometimes hesitant to test. That same hesitancy does not generally extend to people who are not tribal members or those in other locations in the Americas.

The field of genetic genealogy is now 20 years old, meaning that many tribal members and descendants who are not currently enrolled tribal members have tested, providing the community with a growing baseline of information. Many genealogists have proven their connection to Native ancestors using different types of DNA testing, both for themselves and family members.

---

[12] Peopling of the Americas as inferred from ancient genomics, Willerslev et al., *Nature* June 2021 at https://www.nature.com/articles/s41586-021-03499-y

[13] https://www.nps.gov/subjects/nagpra/index.htm

[14] https://en.wikipedia.org/wiki/Native_American_Graves_Protection_and_Repatriation_Act

How Does DNA Testing for Indigenous American Heritage Work?

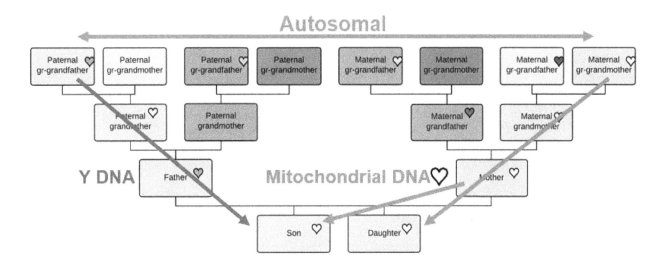

Three types of DNA testing—Y, mitochondrial, and autosomal—can help researchers identify and pinpoint indigenous American ancestors. Y and mitochondrial DNA are never mixed with the DNA of the other parent, so—unlike autosomal DNA—they are passed intact to offspring, generation after generation. Therefore, both Y and mitochondrial DNA can identify specific ancestors as Native regardless of how far back in your tree they are located.

Y and mitochondrial DNA reach much further back in time than autosomal. Different types of DNA serve unique genealogical purposes and allow us to approach the puzzle from different angles.

- Y DNA is inherited by males from their fathers via the Y chromosome, which is always passed from fathers to sons. The Y chromosome is what makes males male. Daughters don't inherit a Y chromosome, and therefore need to ask their father, brother, uncle, or a male descended through all males from the suspected male Native ancestor to take a Y DNA test.

Y DNA is divided into genetically related groups, known as *haplogroups*, which are found in various parts of the world. We know that subsets of haplogroups Q and C are found among the indigenous inhabitants of the Americas.

- Mitochondrial DNA is passed directly from mothers to both sexes of children, but only females pass it on. You inherited your mitochondrial DNA from your mother, who inherited it from her mother, on up the line through direct matrilineal ancestors.

Mitochondrial DNA is also divided into haplogroups, with indigenous American mitochondrial DNA falling into subsets of haplogroups A, B, C, D, and X.

You may not be descended from your Native ancestors in a direct lineal fashion, so to confirm Native heritage you will need to find a family member whose Y or mitochondrial DNA descends appropriately. Later in this book, we'll discuss different ways to find Y and mitochondrial DNA testers, as well as how to determine if someone from your line may have already tested.

While both Y DNA and mitochondrial DNA, sometimes written as mtDNA, descend from one particular line, reaching thousands of years back in time in an unbroken chain to confirm Native heritage, autosomal DNA is different.

- Autosomal DNA is inherited differently than either Y DNA or mitochondrial DNA. Every child inherits half of each of parent's autosomal DNA on chromosomes 1–22, typically known as the autosomes.

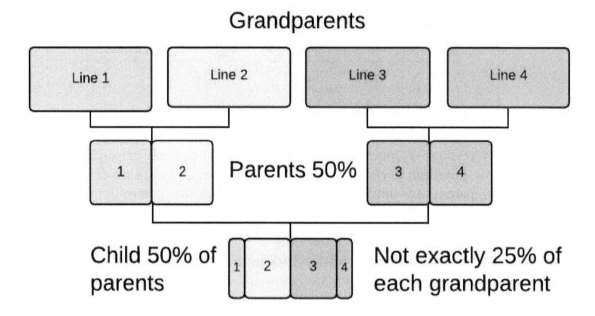

You are made up of exactly 50% of your mother's and 50% of your father's autosomal DNA. However, you do not inherit exactly 25% of each of your grandparents' DNA.

In the graphic above, you can see that the parents inherited half of the autosomal DNA of the grandparents. The paternal grandparents are identified as Line 1 and Line 2, while the maternal grandparents are identified as Line 3 and Line 4. You can also see that the child has exactly 50% of each parent, but not 25% of each grandparent. In our example above, it looks like the tester inherited significantly more of their paternal grandmother's (Line 2) DNA than their paternal grandfather's (Line 1) and more of their maternal grandfather's (Line 3) DNA than their maternal grandmother's (Line 4).

In a real-life example, two grandchildren inherited the following amounts of their four grandparents' DNA.

Grandchild	% Paternal Grandfather	% Paternal Grandmother	% Maternal Grandfather	% Maternal Grandmother
Grandchild 1	26	24	23	27
Grandchild 2	28	22	24	26

While both mitochondrial DNA and Y DNA test only one specific line, reaching back in time indefinitely, autosomal DNA tests all your DNA lines, but not deeply. Think of Y and mtDNA as deep but not broad, and autosomal as broad but not deep.

Autosomal DNA tests about 700,000 locations that are most likely to mutate in human DNA in order to compare those locations with other testers. Of course, the more closely you're related, the more DNA you'll share. The further back in time, the less DNA of a common ancestor you'll share with other testers.

Autosomal DNA is utilized in two ways:

- DNA matching to other testers identifies matches with people that occur in a genealogical time frame, typically within 5 or 6 generations, but sometimes back 10 generations or so. Autosomal DNA is divided in each generation, with each child inheriting half of each parent's DNA. Therefore, half of the ancestral DNA is lost in each generation until discernable DNA from individual ancestors can no longer be identified.

- Ethnicity or population-based estimates can be made.

Of course, matching to other testers can be and is very important to genealogy, but if you're searching for confirmation of Native American ancestors, you'll want to use all the different types of DNA in addition to traditional records.[15] DNA matching may be very important after you identify a Native ancestor, but may not be the most useful tool early in the identification process.

Chromosome 23, the X chromosome, is also inherited differently, with a unique inheritance path. Males only inherit one X chromosome, inherited from their mother, because they receive a Y chromosome from their father instead. This inheritance pattern is reflected throughout the tree, limiting the number of ancestors that your X chromosome can be inherited from.

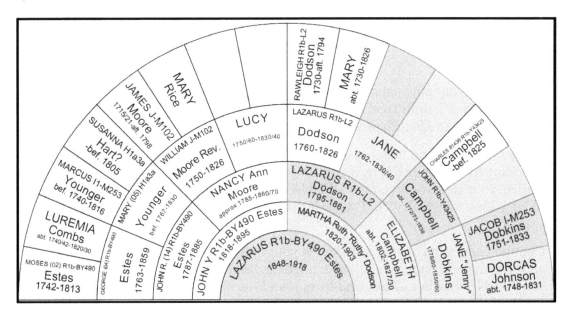

---

[15] https://dna-explained.com/2018/07/11/ancestors-what-constitutes-proof/

Females inherit an X chromosome from their father as well.

The X chromosome is used in the same way as genetic information on chromosomes 1–22, but taking into account its unique inheritance properties. You can read about the X chromosome's unique inheritance path on my blog in the article "Concepts: Inheritance."[16]

It's worth noting that the X chromosome is SNP-poor, meaning that the cM size often needs to be roughly one and a half to two times the size of matches on chromosomes 1–22 to be of the same relevance. For example, if your personal threshold is that you don't use autosomal segments smaller than 7 cM, then an equivalent threshold for the X chromosome would be approximately 10–14 cM.

Not all vendors include X DNA in their results, and Ancestry does not provide segment information at all, so you don't know if they are utilizing X DNA or not.

Tribes

Can DNA Results Identify a Tribe?

The single most common question I receive about DNA testing and Native American heritage is whether the tester can identify a tribe and, if so, join it.

Identifying and joining a tribe is not a simple yes or no question. In other words, "it depends."

First, remember that a tribe is a combination of a cultural community, an extended family, and a legal entity.

You may, and I stress the word *may*, be able to discern several pieces of information based on various types of DNA test results:

- Confirmation through Y and mitochondrial DNA haplogroups that your ancestors were in fact Native.

- Segments of your autosomal DNA identified as Native by either 23andMe's Ancestry Composition or FamilyTreeDNA's myOrigins Chromosome Painting that you can potentially use to identify people who match you on those segments.

- Suggestions based on matches and their known history as to the region where your ancestors lived. For example, if your mitochondrial DNA haplogroup is confirmed to be Native, your closest mitochondrial DNA matches might be clustered in the Pueblo region of New Mexico, which would suggest that area would be a good location to focus your search.

- Common ancestors of your matches. If your matches share a common ancestor with one another, that ancestor, or a relative, might be your ancestor too. For example, if three of your Y DNA matches all descend from John Deer Runner, you might have a connection

---

[16] https://dna-explained.com/category/x-chromosome/

to the John Deer Runner family, or you might not. Build your tree back as far as possible and see if you can find a connection of some sort—either genealogical or geographical.

- Autosomal DNA may lead you to shared ancestors, common regions, matching Native segments, and more.

You will probably need to utilize multiple tools along with traditional genealogical records to reveal specifics.

Sometimes these suggestions or pieces of evidence allow you to focus your research, which will end up resulting in a genealogical breakthrough. For example, research might reveal an ancestor listed in the special Indian Census Rolls enumerated by tribe[17] between 1885 and 1940[18] in a Native family on a reservation. You may also find your Native family member in the regular federal decennial census as well as in various state censuses.[19] Not all states took state censuses, but those that did generally took the census at the five-year marker between the decennial federal census.

DNA alone does not connect you with a specific tribe. Remember that tribal definitions were and are fluid. New tribes often splintered from more-established, larger tribes when the area could no longer support the size of the tribe, or when new opportunities arose nearby, or when conflicts emerged. Those tribes had different names, like neighboring towns do today, but they still shared their common ancestral roots, language, and heritage.

Using Y or mitochondrial DNA results, you can prove or disprove that a specific ancestor had Native roots on a particular direct line. Autosomal cannot, without additional research, confirm a Native connection on any one line.[20]

Ethnicity is only an estimate and may or may not reveal Native heritage accurately, especially with distant ancestors or small amounts of Native American DNA. We'll discuss that in the Ethnicity section in Part 2.

Can I Join a Tribe?

The short answer is "no." A consumer DNA test alone will not qualify you for tribal membership in a federally recognized tribe.[21]

The long answer is that "it's complicated." It's also a chicken-and-egg proposition.

To join a federally recognized tribe in the United States, you will need two things:

- A CDIB (Certificate of Degree of Indian Blood) card, issued by the Bureau of Indian Affairs (BIA)

---

[17] https://accessgenealogy.com/native/free-us-indian-census-rolls.htm

[18] https://www.archives.gov/research/census/native-americans/1885-1940.html

[19] https://www.familysearch.org/wiki/en/United_States_Census_State_Censuses

[20] The exception would be very close relatives. If your parent or grandparent is fully Native, then based on your DNA match to them as expected, your tribal association is proven.

[21] Always check with the tribe in question for specifics.

- Application and admission to the appropriate tribe from which you descend

In order to apply for a CDIB card, you must know the tribe (or tribes) from which you descend and to which your ancestor(s) belonged. On the BIA's website is "A Guide to Tracing American Indian and Alaska Native Ancestry," [22] and numerous other resources are available at www. indianaffairs.gov.

Not all tribes are federally recognized. Some tribes are recognized by states, and yet others are unrecognized and remain community-based organizations.

In some cases, groups have been known to represent themselves as "tribes," granting membership in exchange for application fees. Be quite wary of schemes like this, especially if they also require personal information such as social security number, address, names of family members, and/or a birth certificate. This is not to imply that all tribes that are neither state nor federally recognized fall into this category. However, some groups portraying themselves as "tribes" are opportunistic, preying on people desiring a connection. Tread very carefully and perform thorough research before submitting an application that reveals personal information about you and your family.

It should be noted that legitimate tribes will also ask for this type of information—the difference being that recognized tribes have a decades- or centuries-long status as a tribal entity confirmed by federal or state governments, as well as an established tribal government, and they haven't been constructed by an individual or group of individuals who may have ulterior motives.

If you don't quality for membership in a recognized tribe, you can certainly continue to research your ancestors and learn about their history and culture.

Obtaining a CDIB Card

To obtain a CDIB card, [23] you must complete the application, detailing your amount or degree of Native American "blood" referred to as "blood quantum." [24]

Blood quantum is calculated as the percentage of Native American "blood" you are expected to have based on a particular ancestor who was a member of a federally recognized tribe, and from whom you must unquestionably prove descent.

For example, if one grandparent is fully Native and a tribal member, with a CDIB card and tribal membership number, and your other three grandparents were not Native, your blood quantum would be 25% or one-fourth. However, if that grandparent who was a tribal member was only half Native, your blood quantum would then be 12.5% or one-eighth. You can also descend from multiple tribes, and your CDIB card will reflect your heritage divided among tribes. However, you can only join one tribe.

---

[22] https://www.bia.gov/sites/bia.gov/files/assets/foia/ois/pdf/idc-002619.pdf

[23] https://www.bie.edu/sites/default/files/documents/idc1-029262.pdf

[24] https://www.bia.gov/bia/ois/tgs/genealogy

On the CDIB application,[25] you must provide the following:

- Proof of tribal membership of the ancestor from whom you wish to claim blood lineal descent

- Birth and death certificates of people between you and your confirmed Native ancestor in your family tree

- Maiden names of all females

- Your certified birth certificate

If your parents or grandparents have a CDIB card, you can piggyback from their card, providing their CDIB card number plus documentation as to your descent from them.

Adopted children cannot obtain CDIB cards through adoptive parents.

Native children adopted to non-Native parents can obtain a CDIB card by tracing through their biological parents to the Native ancestor.[26]

After receiving a CDIB card from the federal government, the next step is to apply for membership in the tribe from which you descend.

Every Tribe Has Unique Membership Requirements

Every tribe establishes its own criteria for membership, which varies widely. Specifically, every tribe has its own blood quantum membership requirement, which can vary from 50% to 0%. Blood quantum is only one of several requirements, but if you don't fulfill the blood quantum requirement, that's an immediate showstopper.

Because of the varying tribal blood quantum requirements, it behooves applicants to review the tribal requirements before applying for a CDIB card. If the tribe in question requires one-fourth blood quantum, meaning a grandparent with whom you would share approximately 25% of your DNA, and your closest Native ancestor in your tree is your great-grandparent, meaning you would be one-eighth, or 12.5%, there's no point in applying for your CDIB card if your goal is to qualify for tribal membership.

To be clear, the CDIB card *itself* does not confer any benefits or tribal membership. It does recognize an individual as having some level of proven Native American heritage. Benefits are conferred upon tribal members only, and obtaining the CDIB card is just the first step in the tribal membership process.

In the United States, there were a total of 562 federally recognized American Indian Tribes and Alaska Natives[27] as of January 2021. Various tribes continue to apply for recognition, so that

---

[25] https://www.bia.gov/sites/bia.gov/files/assets/public/raca/online_forms/pdf/Certificate_of_Degree_of_Indian_Blood_1076-0153_Exp3-31-21_508.pdf

[26] https://narf.org/nill/documents/icwa/faq/access.html

[27] https://www.federalregister.gov/documents/2020/01/30/2020-01707/indian-entities-recognized-by-and-eligible-to-receive-services-from-the-united-states-bureau-of

number will increase over time. Criteria for a tribe to become federally recognized[28] includes, minimally, that it must

- be a distinct autonomous community;
- be recognized as such since before 1900;
- have existed as such since historical times;
- have political influence over its members; and
- have membership criteria.

An individual who wishes to join a tribe must first identify the appropriate tribe, then refer to the Tribal Leaders Directory,[29] which provides tribal leader contact information, websites, and other links. Applicants will need to contact the tribe, requesting its criteria for tribal membership. You may be able to find information more quickly by googling "tribal membership requirements" for the specific tribe. Just be sure that you're referencing the actual tribe's official site, not something else.

You can expect requirements for membership to be some combination of the following:

- Blood quantum requirement, possibly varying by birth year
- Requirement that applicants descend from a particular earlier tribal membership roll or rolls
- Not being a member of any other tribe
- Language, meaning that you speak the Native language
- Driver's license or state ID card
- Notarized statement
- Physical description, including height, weight, natural hair color, natural eye color, and sex
- Social security number
- Residence requirements, such as living on reservations, pueblos or rancherias, or associated "tribal trust lands" for the current or recent generations
- Continuous communication and cultural affiliation with the tribe or tribal members
- Recognition of the applicant within the community as Native
- Requirement to pick up card in person at the tribal office
- Possibly additional requirements

---

[28] https://en.wikipedia.org/wiki/Native_American_recognition_in_the_United_States
[29] https://www.federalregister.gov/documents/2020/01/30/2020-01707/indian-entities-recognized-by-and-eligible-to-receive-services-from-the-united-states-bureau-of

The process of enrollment in a Native American tribe has historical roots that extend back to the early nineteenth century. As the US government dispossessed native peoples of their lands and property, treaties established specific rights, privileges, goods, and money to which those who were party to a treaty—both tribes as entities and individual tribal members—were entitled.

The practices of creating formal censuses and keeping lists of names of tribal members originated to ensure all "Indians" were removed from their lands. Later, tribal rolls evolved when tribes began keeping their own rolls and census information in order to provide an accurate and equitable distribution of benefits among members.[30]

While some tribes have tightened their restrictions, others have moved in the other direction, recognizing membership as a political relationship, available to descendants of Native people who have been urbanized, intermarried outside the tribe, and moved away.

With each successive generation, unless the Native person or descendant marries another tribal member, the amount of blood quantum is halved, and eventually fewer and fewer individuals qualify to be tribal members, even if they live on the reservation. Ultimately, many are no longer eligible to enroll, regardless of where they live.

For those individuals who know or think that they have Native American heritage, who have been disenfranchised from their tribe or tribes during the genocidal history of the settlement of the Americas, this approach may seem incredibly unfair. It helps to look at it from the tribal members' perspective.

Life on the Reservation

Tribal members who remain on reservations as residents live with the effects of generations of debilitating poverty. They experience substandard living environments in remote areas where neither education nor jobs are readily available and are in desperate need of the treaty services, including food, available to tribal members.

For example, the Lakota Sioux Pine Ridge Indian Reservation[31] in South Dakota where the Wounded Knee Massacre took place on December 29, 1890,[32] has both the lowest average life expectancy (66 years) and the lowest per capita income ($7,773) of any county or reservation in the country. The unemployment rate is 89%, not because tribal members are unwilling to work, but because there are no jobs available on the reservation. The poverty rate is over 53%, compared to the national average of 15.6%.[33]

In 2011 Diane Sawyer visited the Pine Ridge Indian Reservation for a documentary about life on the reservation, titled *Hidden America: Children of the Plains*. I highly recommend watching this series

---

[30] https://www.ncbi.nlm.nih.gov/books/NBK233104/#:~:text=The%20Bureau%20of%20Indian%20Affairs%20uses%20a%20blood%20quantum%20definition,membership%20(enrollment)%20of%20individuals.

[31] https://en.wikipedia.org/wiki/Pine_Ridge_Indian_Reservation

[32] https://en.wikipedia.org/wiki/Wounded_Knee_Massacre

[33] https://www.re-member.org/pine-ridge-reservation.aspx

to appreciate tribal life as it actually exists today.[34] Life on the reservation is not a glorified spiritual existence, but a daily and lifelong battle for survival. Many people simply don't survive, and no family is untouched by tragedy.

This series will help those who don't live on the reservation understand why the tribes don't need or want additional members. The tribes and tribal members already don't have nearly enough resources.

I have to confess that I can barely watch these documentaries revealing generations of the most abject poverty I've ever witnessed. It's not limited to the Pine Ridge Reservation—they are but one of many.

Multigenerational homes are the norm, meaning that the Covid pandemic has ravaged our indigenous communities. The Navajo Nation had the highest Covid-19 Delta infection rate, per capita, in the United States as of September 2021.

Benefits and Services

Benefits and services such as the following are provided to tribal members as a result of treaties signed with tribes by the government:

- Educational aid
- Potential for tuition-free or reduced-cost college
- Eligibility for some scholarships
- Health care
- Food subsidies
- Land allotments
- Housing on tribal lands
- Royalties from the sale of resources
- Distributions of tribal funds, including casinos

Tribal members and recent descendants who desperately need resources resent the people who have no contemporary or recent connection to the tribe and only want to join to obtain benefits allocated to or reserved for tribal members. In some cases, the total "pie" is split among enrolled tribal members, meaning the more members, the smaller the slice for each member.

The Diane Sawyer documentary illustrates that the "free services" and housing are incredibly substandard, condemning generation after generation to bone-crushing poverty.

---

[34] *Hidden America: Children of the Plains* Part 1/5 https://www.youtube.com/watch?v=IJapHc7B8Xs; Part 2/5 https://www.youtube.com/watch?v=J6sdTOO_uxo; Part 3/5 https://www.youtube.com/watch?v=R2x4s4SLj4o; Part 4/5 https://www.youtube.com/watch?v=dc94YDtSM1E; Part 5/5 https://www.youtube.com/watch?v=JCqL9qcwVMU

History Informs Today's Research?

Removing the financial incentive from the equation, many people simply want to connect with their tribe and reconnect with a birthright they feel was unjustly stolen from them and their family through no fault or actions of their own. Genealogists who are thrilled to finally connect the dots find rejection by the tribes and outspoken tribal members both disappointing and hurtful. This leaves genealogists feeling that although their ancestors suffered and managed to survive attempted genocide, they themselves—having finally found their way back home—have been soundly rejected by their distant family, who wants nothing to do with them.

In many families, Native roots never disappeared entirely. Proud stories about Native ancestors have remained. Healing practices and other cultural remnants are buried in family practices that aren't specifically attributed to Native heritage but have their roots there just the same. There was no "proof" of being Native or descending from Native ancestors back then because proof wasn't needed. Not only was proof not needed, it was not desirable.

In many parts of the country, Native people and their descendants were not legally considered "white," and therefore discriminatory practices discouraged admitting to "Native" ancestors for fear of reprisal. Native American heritage was whispered about and passed from generation to generation privately.

Native Americans weren't allowed to be citizens until 1924, when President Calvin Coolidge signed into law the Indian Citizenship Act,[35] even though in 1870 the Native population[36] exceeded that of 5 states and 10 territories.[37] Noncitizens can't vote in US elections, and some Indians couldn't vote until the passage of the 1964 and 1965 Civil and Voting Rights Acts.

Additionally, powwows and Native American religious practices[38] were banned until President Jimmy Carter signed the American Indian Religious Freedom Act[39] on August 11, 1978.[40] The powwows I attended as a child, and even those I took my children to before and after 1978, were all held in hidden locations, far from prying eyes.

I danced at a powwow in early August 1978 to celebrate a family event, and although the people attending knew that the bill was likely to be signed, no one actually believed it would end discrimination. One of the dancers proudly affirmed, "We dance for our ancestors, with or without any law." Native people weren't allowed to speak their own language, and children were forced to be educated and tested in English until 1990 with the passing of the Native American Languages Act.[41]

---

[35] https://www.archives.gov/historical-docs/todays-doc/?dod-date=602

[36] https://www.archives.gov/publications/prologue/2006/summer/indian-census.html

[37] https://constitutioncenter.org/blog/on-this-day-in-1924-all-indians-made-united-states-citizens

[38] https://www.nationalgeographic.org/article/native-americans-and-freedom-religion/

[39] https://coast.noaa.gov/data/Documents/OceanLawSearch/Summary%20of%20Law%20-%20American%20Indian%20Religious%20Freedom%20Act.pdf

[40] https://en.wikipedia.org/wiki/American_Indian_Religious_Freedom_Act

[41] https://en.wikipedia.org/wiki/Native_American_Languages_Act_of_1990

Conversely—given the effects of slavery, Indian removal from lands east of the Mississippi in the 1830s,[42] and the Jim Crow era—if one could pass for "Indian" instead of black, that was preferable. Often people were (and even now are) forced to select one checkbox for "race." The "white" box was always safest, followed by "Indian" if you had to claim something else. It's no wonder we've lost the trail back into the past.

Land

The removal of American Indians from their homelands began not long after Europeans first began settling these shores. The first reservation was established in 1786, and the constant arrival of new settlers pushed the Native people further and further westward—and certainly not peaceably.[43] Treaties were made and broken,[44] reservations established, and rations given to compensate the Native people for stripping away not only their lands but also their hunting grounds and ability to provide for themselves.[45]

Culminating with the Indian Removal Act of 1830,[46] entire tribes were forcibly relocated to what was at that time considered to be wasteland so that white men could settle, without a fight, the desirable land that the Indian tribes still occupied. This relocation, known as the "Trail of Tears,"[47] was held during the dead of winter, an intentional genocidal act designed to kill as many Native people as possible.

While we often think of the Five Civilized Tribes[48]—Cherokee, Creek, Chickasaw, Choctaw, and Seminole—as the primary tribes relocated to Indian Territory, there were a total of 65 tribes forced into Indian Territory, now Oklahoma.[49]

Beginning in the 1870s and reaching into the early 1900s, when the federal government began to divide communally held tribal lands into individually owned private property,[50] descendants who legitimately had settled or married out of the tribe but had Native ancestors applied for their share—but so did many people who opportunistically "remembered" Native ancestors where none existed.

The tribes most affected by this land allocation policy were the tribes removed in the 1830s to what would eventually become Oklahoma.[51] This is likely the genesis of many of the "Cherokee Indian Princess" stories we still hear today. Fortunately for genealogists, the Enrollment Jackets,

---

[42] https://en.wikipedia.org/wiki/Indian_Removal_Act
[43] https://www.loc.gov/classroom-materials/immigration/native-american/removing-native-americans-from-their-land/
[44] https://en.wikipedia.org/wiki/List_of_United_States_treaties
[45] https://www.npr.org/sections/codeswitch/2015/01/18/368559990/broken-promises-on-display-at-native-american-treaties-exhibit
[46] https://en.wikipedia.org/wiki/Indian_Removal_Act
[47] https://en.wikipedia.org/wiki/Trail_of_Tears
[48] https://en.wikipedia.org/wiki/Five_Civilized_Tribes
[49] https://www.familysearch.org/wiki/en/Indigenous_Peoples_of_Oklahoma
[50] https://www.ourdocuments.gov/doc.php?flash=false&doc=50&page=transcript
[51] https://www.okhistory.org/publications/enc/entry.php?entry=AL011

known as Dawes Applications or Testimonial Packets, still exist and often provide a treasure trove of information.[52]

The tribes that had been relocated to "Indian Territory" were not the only tribes involved with land allocation. In fact, the Dawes Act initially excluded these tribes, but later included them. Members of the Lakota Sioux—and other tribes with members over whom the government acted paternalistically, giving them meager annuities and food that assured the continued status of poverty—were to be granted between 30 and 120 acres of land individually. The rationalization for this was that if each person was motivated to succeed individually, no longer having to be subservient to the government, they would be able to live better lives and would more rapidly drop their Indian way of life, with nothing holding them fast to the reservation. However, the Pine Ridge Reservation[53] land is not conducive to farming, and most Lakota could not even eke out a subsistence living from the land.

As time passed, more people did leave their ancestral homelands, whether by force or choice. With cultural assimilation came disconnection—and eventually all that was left were fleeting memories and a few stories. Today, it's up to genealogy and perhaps DNA to disclose and confirm Native ancestry for those who have become disconnected from ancestors who left or were displaced.

First Nations in Canada

The Canadian government recognizes 634 First Nations bands who are similar to tribes in the United States, although the membership criteria is different. These bands comprise more than 2% of Canadian residents.

Like in the United States, benefits are both valuable and variable,[54] and who should and should not be recognized is a widely debated political hot-potato. Some bands determine their own membership, and some do not.

You can determine if you may be eligible to join by contacting the Indigenous Services Department.[55] The Canadian Indian Services Act[56] is complex and confusing, but in general, one parent or an immediate family member—such as an uncle, aunt, or cousin—will need to have already been issued a Certificate of Indian Status card. You will also need to know the band to which you are eligible to belong before applying.

---

[52] https://www.archives.gov/research/native-americans/dawes/dawes-enrollment.html

[53] https://en.wikipedia.org/wiki/Pine_Ridge_Indian_Reservation

[54] https://www.sac-isc.gc.ca/eng/1100100032472/1572459733507

[55] https://www.sac-isc.gc.ca/eng/1462808207464/1572460627149

[56] https://laws-lois.justice.gc.ca/eng/acts/i-5/

Cultural Appropriation

What a well-meaning genealogist may view as cultural appreciation and learning about the various aspects of their heritage may be viewed as cultural appropriation by others, both within and outside of the tribes. It's a bit confusing, so let me explain.

Cultural appropriation is when a custom, act, or behavior is associated with a particular culture, particularly one that is not powerful—and members of the powerful culture take it over or engage in it as their own.[57]

For example, Native-related activities—including donning regalia, dancing at powwows, or in some cases, even sharing stories and simply researching Native heritage—are perceived by some people today as engaging in cultural appropriation.

Here's an example. I visited the Caribbean about 20 years ago. My hair is long and thick. Women who live there were soliciting tourists to braid their hair into cornrows. I gladly accepted and paid a lovely Caribbean woman to perform that service for me—and I was much more comfortable during my visit. However, cornrow braids are found in their culture but are not part of mine.

Did I engage in cultural appropriation and, if so, was that inappropriate behavior on my part? I don't know. It never occurred to me at the time, especially given the solicitation. If so, I certainly didn't mean it as such. In hindsight, could someone today perceive it as such? Even if that had been a genealogy trip to find my ancestors? Certainly, someone could.

Conversely, the women soliciting the tourists viewed hair braiding as a positive factor, providing themselves with an income opportunity. I appreciated their culture, enjoyed the experience, and infused money into their economy. Would they view my actions as appropriating their culture under those circumstances? Probably not.

Of course, genealogists seeking a Native ancestor do not view their course of action as appropriating anything that isn't theirs. In fact, exactly the opposite is true. They see the search and resulting identification of Native ancestors as reclaiming something that **is** inherently theirs and was stolen from them through genocidal policies and actions.

Genealogists see heartwarming stories about African American people who discover their African tribal roots, return to Africa, and are welcomed with open arms.[58] In 2019 Jay Speights, an interfaith pastor from Maryland, returned to Benin, arriving to be greeted with a sign that said, "Welcome to the kingdom of Allada, land of your ancestors." He was treated as royalty, literally a descendant of a King, and given a new name ("Videkon Deka," the child who came back) before leaving at the end of two weeks. Yet, Native researchers are not received in the same way and are

---

[57] https://www.theatlantic.com/entertainment/archive/2015/10/the-dos-and-donts-of-cultural-appropriation/411292/

[58] https://www.washingtonpost.com/local/im-a-prince-after-years-of-searching-for-family-history-a-pastor-discovers-royal-ties-to-africa/2019/02/21/47238d0a-316e-11e9-86ab-5d02109aeb01_story.html

often shunned for reasons we have already mentioned—very different receptions to two groups who have both had their historical umbilical cord to their ancestors severed.

While activities can be perceived differently, there is wide agreement that some acts are offensive to people of a specific culture. For example, Native people would find a non-Native person wearing a Native American war bonnet made of eagle feathers, an item that holds a designated earned status and significance to tribal members, extremely offensive. Eagle feathers are considered sacred by many tribes.[59]

Dance regalia at powwows is not a "costume" and is handmade for and by each dancer. Powwows are sacred, spiritual, community events, and while visitors are usually welcome to attend, each tribe decides who can dance, often by dance type. Powwows vary widely by region and tribe, and the etiquette is different with each one.[60]

Some tribes only allow dancing by their tribal members, some welcome other tribal members, some include people who carry CDIB cards, and some invite everyone to dance in "intertribal" dances, even those who are not a member of any tribe and not wearing regalia.[61] If intertribal dancing is welcomed, an announcement inviting people to join the dance circle is made before those specific dances. Certain traditions and rituals are observed relative to feathers; photography; the drums and drummers, known collectively as "the Drum"; and other items and customs.

While those examples are clear, there's a lot of gray area. There is no line in the sand, nor general agreement about this topic. If you're going to attend a powwow, research the expected etiquette and watch other people for cues. Ask if you're unsure, especially about photography. It's always a good idea to familiarize yourself with local tribal customs before attending events.

I'm not advising you about what is culturally appropriate or how to behave, simply alerting you to tread carefully lest you unintentionally offend someone and/or become a target for online ridicule. Don't expect to be welcomed with open arms by your long-lost Native family. A Native academic several years ago stated that it's not enough to "claim" a tribal affiliation, they must "claim you back." That opinion is widely quoted but is not universally held.

Educating yourself in advance about the tribe and culture is the best way to be respectful.

There are centuries of unpleasant history based on the treatment of the Native people by the dominant culture throughout the Americas. That history isn't all in the past and continues to dramatically affect tribes and their members today. It's no wonder those rivers of pain run so deep.

Perhaps, as genealogists, we want to be that happy ending, to avenge and honor those ancestors who were so terribly wronged—to find our way back to them so we can raise them from obscurity, celebrate their life, learn their culture, and show that while they may have suffered depredations and defeats, that does not extend to exterminating and extinguishing their descendants' Native

---

[59] https://blog.nativehope.org/the-feather-symbol-of-high-honor
[60] https://en.wikipedia.org/wiki/Pow_wow
[61] https://www.powwows.com/pow-wow-101-frequently-asked-questions-native-american-pow-wows/

blood and pride in their heritage. They gave us life. They are in us. From a genealogist's perspective, that's not cultural appropriation.

That's long-awaited justice, combined with ancestral pride.

Family Stories

The first thing researchers seeking Native ancestors can do is narrow down the potential family lines where Native heritage may be found.

Talk to older relatives. Ask about letters written by those who have passed on. Ask other people who may recall different pieces of information. In my family, letters written by both my grandfather and my father indicate that our supposed Native ancestor was my father's paternal grandmother, or her mother. They were mentioned in multiple letters as Cherokee.

At the time Native ancestry was first mentioned in my family, I didn't know anything about either woman, including their names. I knew that the family lived in Claiborne County, Tennessee.

I had no reason to suspect that this information was incorrect, so I believed it. The older generation, my aunts, provided additional tidbits of information, "confirming" the information reflected in those letters. What they confirmed is that they had heard the same stories, not that the stories were accurate.

As I began to actively research, I discovered that my father's paternal grandmother, Elizabeth Vannoy, was born in 1847 in Hancock County, Tennessee, near the Virginia line. While the Cherokee did live in parts of Tennessee, they did not live in that area.

No matter, it must have been her mother, right?

Marriage records showed that Phebe, Elizabeth's mother, born in 1818, had married in 1845 in Claiborne County, the portion that eventually become Hancock County. The year 1818 was before the removal, and still, Phebe and her family were not living in an area where any Native people were living.

I still believed the information because it had been provided by family members, spread across two older generations, who all knew much more about the family than I did. My grandfather was born in 1874. Elizabeth was his mother, and Phebe, his grandmother, lived until he was 27 years old. He knew these people!

It took a few years to track this line back another generation, which was much more elusive. I was dealing with burned courthouses, along with the fact that I had no idea where the family had come "from" before Claiborne/Hancock County. It was easy to interpret the fact that I had a difficult time finding Phebe's parents as evidence that they were Native and living among the tribe, but that wasn't the case.

However, DNA testing came along before I definitively proved the identity of Phebe's mother through traditional records. If either Elizabeth or her mother, Phebe, were fully Native American, as had been stated, their mitochondrial DNA would fall into the haplogroups carried by Native

Americans. If they were only Native on their direct matrilineal line, that would also be reflected in their mitochondrial DNA.

I found an individual who descended from Phebe through Elizabeth through all females who agreed to take the mitochondrial DNA test. Their haplogroup, J1c2c, is definitely not Native.

Could only the father of one of those women have been Native, which would explain why their mitochondrial, or matrilineal, DNA was not Native? Yes, of course, but I had records placing both Phebe and Elizabeth's fathers in non-Native areas too, and the census indicated "white." Often, in mixed marriages, the man was white or non-Native and the wife was Native.

Eventually, I tested the Y DNA of Elizabeth and Phebe's husbands through descendants, and they weren't Native either. I traced their lines back several more generations, and no Native American ancestors emerged.

I was confused.

What I did find, however, was that Elizabeth's brother and several of Elizabeth's children had gone to Oklahoma and settled in what had been Indian Territory. Her brother bought land that had been allocated to a Native man. My father's paternal great-grandfather had left his family in Tennessee in the 1870s, walked to Oklahoma, and was living on Choctaw land until his death in 1898.

Had these stories somehow morphed into Native American ancestry? Did "someone" have Native ancestry, but it wasn't in our direct line? Was it possible that the migration of several family members to Oklahoma had been viewed as "confirmation" by earlier generations?

When autosomal testing became available, three of Elizabeth's grandchildren were available for testing, as were several great-grandchildren. If Elizabeth was fully Native, her grandchildren would have been expected to show approximately 25% Native ethnicity. If Elizabeth was half-Native, the grandchildren would have approximately 12.5%. While this amount would not be exact, those descendants would not be expected to show none. A few showed small amounts of Native American ancestry, but remember, they also carried the DNA of several other ancestors who are not related to either Elizabeth or me.

Two of the testers who did show Native Ancestry also descended through a common grandmother, and ironically, it was through that line—not through Elizabeth, where it was originally reported—that they found and tracked Native heritage, much further back in time.

I also eventually discovered completely by accident that I carried Native heritage through my mother's ancestors. She and I both carry Native autosomal DNA segments that track back to Acadian ancestors from Nova Scotia who are proven Native by both Y and mitochondrial DNA.

You may find that the lines you expect to be Native are not, and you may discover entirely unexpected results in a different line. Testing relatives is critically important for two reasons:

- They inherited DNA from your ancestors that you did not.

- Multiple relatives may have inherited the same segment of DNA from ancestors that can be proven to be Native.

- Some relatives may have inherited the Y or mitochondrial DNA of those ancestors, which can unquestionably confirm or refute Native ancestry on that specific line.

What Is and Isn't Proof?

It's important to stress the following:

- The lack of DNA proof does *not* disprove Native ancestry. Absence of evidence is not evidence of absence. It only means you're going to have to look for other types of evidence, such as autosomal DNA in other family members who share only your ancestors, like parents or aunts and uncles, or Y/mitochondrial DNA evidence.

- The presence of small amounts of autosomal DNA ancestry does not prove Native ancestry. Trace amounts can be "noise" or from a different line entirely.

- An unquestionably Native mitochondrial DNA result from a full sequence DNA test, available today only at FamilyTreeDNA, or a Y DNA test that includes SNP (Single Nucleotide Polymorphism) testing to confirm a Native American haplogroup, would both be proof of Native ancestry.

Ethnicity tests can be good indicators, but many people purchase ethnicity or population-based origin tests only to be disappointed. Ethnicity testing is one type of autosomal DNA testing.

The Genealogical Proof Standard, known as the GPS, requires research, evidence, interpretation, a reasonably exhaustive search, and a conclusion supported by citations and evidence. Every effort should be made to include DNA in every genealogical proof standard argument where possible.

A discussion of ethnicity and the various types of ethnicity tests is included in Part 2 of this book.

PART 2:

ETHNICITY AND POPULATION GENETICS

Ethnicity, Biogeographic Ancestry, Populations, and Communities

Ethnicity

Everyone wants a shortcut, and I'm no different. Consumers often take an autosomal DNA test that includes ethnicity results with the goal of proving their Native ancestry, and with the expectation that they will be able to identify their ancestor and "find their tribe." When no Native ethnicity is reported, many people are terribly disappointed and give up.

Those who do receive Native results and aren't genealogists are sometimes disappointed to learn that Native ethnicity results don't point directly to a specific tribe.

The first thing that we need to understand is how much of your Native ancestor can you expect to inherit.

How Much of Them Is in Me?

As discussed earlier, while everyone inherits exactly half of each parent's autosomal DNA on chromosomes 1–22, you don't inherit exactly 25% of your grandparents' DNA. However, we use that as an approximation because as a group, an average is the best we can do.

Using the expectation that, on average, the DNA of each ancestor is halved in each generation, you can expect to inherit about 6.25% of your great-great-grandparent's DNA (see chart at the top of the next page).

Generation	Relationship	How Many?	DNA %	Birth Year
7	GGGGG-grandparents	128	0.78	1750
6	GGGG-grandparents	64	1.56	1780
5	GGG-grandparents	32	3.12	1810
4	GG-grandparents	16	6.25	1840
3	Great-Grandparents	8	12.5	1870
2	Grandparents	4	25	1900
1	Parents	2	50	1930
	You	1	100	1960

The amount of DNA that you inherit from an ancestor born in 1750, using a 30-year average generation, shrinks to just under 1%. By the time you reach sixth- and seventh-generation ancestors, assuming you inherit any of their DNA at all in recognizable quantities, you're in the trace range of all the vendors.

If your ancestor born in 1750 was entirely Native, with no admixture, and you do in fact inherit .78% of their DNA, that would equate to approximately 26 cM of DNA. That's not a trivial segment of DNA, but the challenge is that it's unlikely you inherited their DNA in one large segment. It's much more likely to be chopped up in smaller segments, some of which may not be able to be recognized as Native due to their size and other factors. Remember, you may not have inherited any discernible DNA from an ancestor seven generations back in time.

To put things in perspective, the Indian Removal occurred between 1830 and 1835, and by that time, many Native people east of the Mississippi were significantly admixed. The Cherokee Chief during the relocation, James Vann, was himself the son of a mixed mother and a white trader father.[62]

Your Native ancestor may not have been fully Native, which means you may have less Native DNA than you would expect, or none at all.

How is Native DNA determined or recognized in your DNA? How do we know what DNA is Native and what came from another population? How does this work?

The answer is found in Population Genetics.

---

[62] https://en.wikipedia.org/wiki/James_Vann

Population Genetics

Population genetics is the study of genetics within specific population groups around the world—meaning how they are alike and how they are collectively different from other population groups.

The term most commonly used today is ethnicity, but the actual definition of ethnicity refers to someone who is a member of a social group of common national or cultural traditions. Race is typically biological, and both terms have been intermixed and confused for years.

Dr. Doug McDonald developed what is known as BGA, or Biogeographical Analysis (sometimes called Biogeographical Ancestry),[63] software. BGA is the estimation of one's biological, ethnic, or geographical origins based on identical sequences of DNA at a particular address that is more prevalent within a given population. The term BGA never caught on.

The primary vendors use the following terms to describe people's percentages of ethnicity/population origins:

- 23andMe—Ancestry Composition, ancestral breakdown of 45 populations

- Ancestry—Ethnicity Estimate for geographic regions and also for Genetic Communities (1,400+ geographies reported, combined between both features)

- MyHeritage—Ethnicity Estimate and Genetic Groups (42 ethnicities, 2,114 Genetic Groups reported)

- FamilyTreeDNA—myOrigins,[64] ancestral breakdown and painting of 90 population clusters

Unfortunately, other terms never became widely adopted in a generic sense, so we will be using the terms "ethnicity," "populations," and "origins" because that's how these results are widely known.

How Does Population Genetics Work?

A cluster of markers, or a genetic sequence, let's say AAAAAAAAAA at a particular genetic address, is found in a specific population 90% of the time, and in the rest of the world's population between 0%–10% of the time. Let's call the population where this sequence is found 90% of the time "the Blue Finnish People."

Therefore, when a testing company discovers AAAAAAAAAA at that location for a customer, they infer that the customer may be related to the Blue Finnish People and classify them as such. Keep in mind that there's a 10% chance that classification is wrong, assuming the DNA segment descends from one parent and is not a result of random recombination.

---

[63] https://dna-explained.com/2012/09/09/doug-mcdonald-on-biogeograpical-analysis/;
https://isogg.org/wiki/Biogeographical_ancestry
[64] https://blog.familytreedna.com/wp-content/uploads/2021/08/myOrigins_3_WhitePaper.pdf

Of course, the Blue Finnish People's segment of DNA may be found in multiple geographies. Let's say this population originated in Europe and is found most frequently today in Finland, followed by Lithuania and Russia.[65] In other words, the population settled in regions that today fall into different, multiple countries.

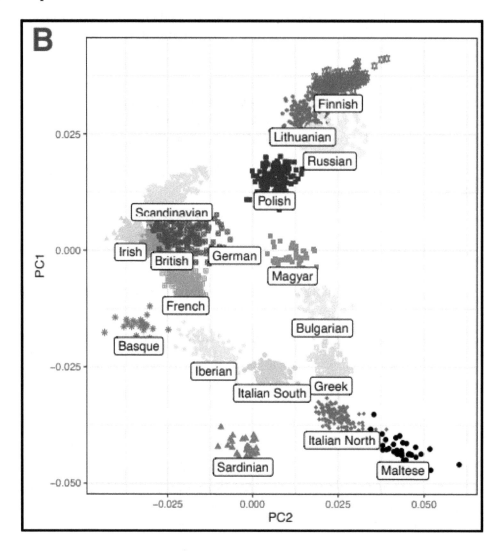

You can see that the PCA (Principal Component Analysis) graphic above shows Finnish at the top, closely related and overlapping with the Lithuanian and Russian populations. Of course, a vendor might assign the tester to the Finnish group, but the tester's ancestor might actually be Lithuanian or Russian, or maybe even Polish, where the segment is found but in slightly lower average frequencies. Of course, the tester could also belong to any other region where the segment frequency is found at 10% or less, as described.

---

[65] PCA plot image, Figure B, courtesy FamilyTreeDNA myOrigins 3.0 white paper at
https://blog.familytreedna.com/wp-content/uploads/2021/08/myOrigins_3_WhitePaper.pdf

Keep in mind when people are upset because vendors can't reliably differentiate between British, Irish, Scottish, Scandinavian, and DNA from continental Europe how similar those populations really are. Not only did the people in England originate from all of those locations, back and forth engagement between the populations has been maintained ever since.

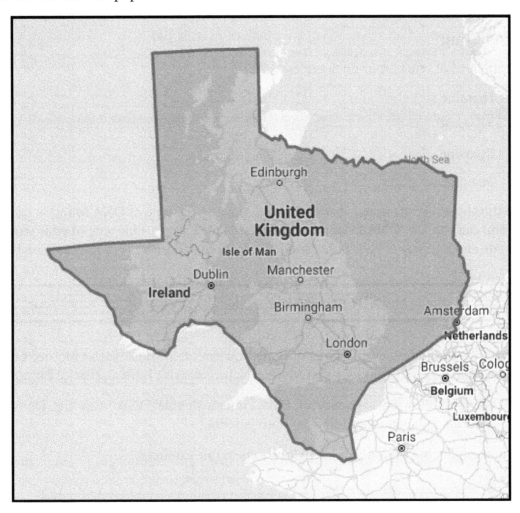

Furthermore, the state of Texas has more land mass than all the British Isles combined, and Ireland is about the size of the state of Indiana.[66]

Next, let's say the Blue Finnish People settled heavily in New Hampshire and a pocket then removed to Louisiana. The Blue Finnish People would be the assigned population or ethnicity, and matching clusters of people would likely be found in diaspora locations too.

So, groups of the Blue Finnish People would be shown together in New Hampshire and Louisiana in the Genetic Communities (Ancestry) and Genetic Groups (MyHeritage) features.

---

[66] Map courtesy of thetruesize.com

These two types of tools—one representing an "origin, ethnicity, or population" location (Finland) and one representing where people of similar DNA are located together more recently (New Hampshire and Louisiana)—are intended to be used together to gain insights.

However, there's a slight twist. Of course!

Parental Phasing

DNA is composed of one of four nucleotides:

- T – Thymine
- A – Adenine
- C – Cytosine
- G - Guanine

You'll see the abbreviations noted above when referencing the type of DNA found in each specific location. You can think of DNA locations as addresses on a street. One side of your street is your mother's side and one side is your father's side—except the addresses are the same on both sides.

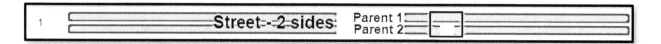

By looking at just the addresses or segments alone, you can't tell which is your mother's nucleotide and which is your father's. Who says that Mother Nature doesn't have a sense of humor!

Let's compare the following sequence of Blue Finnish People DNA with the DNA at those individual locations that you inherited from both parents.

The Blue Finnish People have A's in all 10 locations in our example.

	#1	#2	#3	#4	#5	#6	#7	#8	#9	#10
Blue People - 90%	A	A	A	A	A	A	A	A	A	A
Mom	T	T	T	T	T	A	A	A	A	A
Dad	A	A	A	A	A	C	C	C	C	C

You can see the different DNA in each of the bolded locations that you inherited from your mother and father, respectively. You have two strands of DNA, of course, one from your mother and one from your father, but DNA from those strands has been unwound from the strands during processing in the lab, so DNA companies don't know which of your two nucleotides at each address originated with your mother or father.

You inherited the bolded A's from both parents, so you have 10 contiguous A's—just like the Blue Finnish People.

However, you don't have 10 A's in a row because one of your parents is related to the Blue Finnish People—but because you inherited some of your A's by chance from your mother and some from your father, separately. In genetic genealogy parlance, this is called identical by chance (IBC).[67] That means you don't match someone else or a reference panel, like the Blue Finnish People, due to inheritance or descent. You match because the roll of the dice dictated that you have A's in some locations contributed by each parent. They just happen to be contiguous addresses and just happen to match the Blue Finnish People at that same address. It's the luck of the draw.

Neither your mother's DNA nor your father's DNA match the DNA segment of the Blue Finnish People.

Separating out the DNA that you inherited from each parent is called parentally "phasing your DNA." Unfortunately, because of how your DNA is stored on the double helix, you can't determine which parent each nucleotide of DNA came from without mathematically reassembling the sequence in one of two ways based on the following:

- Which bases, or nucleotides, are most likely to be found together

- Having one or both of your parents test so the parental source or "side" of your DNA at every location can be determined

Of course, the easiest and most straightforward way to phase is by testing your parents. Unfortunately, that's not always possible for any variety of reasons.

When initially processed, instead of seeing the phased DNA, like in the chart above, what the lab sees is something like the following raw data. You have two strands, but the DNA from those strands is combined at each location, in no order.

	#1	#2	#3	#4	#5	#6	#7	#8	#9	#10
Blue People - 90%	A	A	A	A	A	A	A	A	A	A
You	A	T	T	A	T	A	C	C	A	A
You	T	A	A	T	A	C	A	A	C	C

The DNA from both of your strands is intermingled, and we don't know which parent it came from.

There's an AT at location 1, and a TA at location 2—but since the data isn't phased yet, there's no way of knowing which parent the DNA originated with, or if those A's all actually fit together and were inherited from one parent.

I've bolded the A's, so you can see that indeed you do match the Blue Finnish People reference population, but it's not because you share a population or ethnicity with them. It's because you just happened to inherit that sequence of DNA at those locations from different parents. So

---

[67] https://dna-explained.com/2016/03/10/concepts-identical-bydescent-state-population-and-chance/

technically you match, but it's not relevant because it didn't descend from either parent. In other words, your DNA is identical by chance.

	#1	#2	#3	#4	#5	#6	#7	#8	#9	#10
Blue People - 90%	A	A	A	A	A	A	A	A	A	A
Mom	A	A	A	A	A	A	A	A	A	A
Dad	T	T	T	T	T	C	C	C	C	C

In this next example, your mother has tested too. Your DNA is phased against your parents, and your mother contributed all 10 contiguous locations of A. The vendor can then compare segments of DNA (that are in reality a lot longer than 10 contiguous locations) to reference populations around the world in order to determine which populations you match most closely on various portions of your DNA.

Therefore, the more "different" populations are, the easier they are to tell apart. This explains why it's easier to tease apart ethnicities when testers come from highly divergent geographical areas, like continents, where their common ancestors have been separated for tens or hundreds of thousands of years.

While having both parents test is best, what happens if one parent tests, but not the other?

If your father tests and we discover that he has no A's at locations 1–10, we know the A's were inherited from your mother. We can determine the missing parent's nucleotide values by simple subtraction.

- You have AT.
- Your Dad has T.
- Subtract T from AT.
- Therefore, your mother must have the A that remains.

DNA tends to pair with specific other nucleotides.

- T almost always pairs with A.
- C almost always pairs with G.

Sometimes neither parent can test. Scientists can still assemble your nucleotides into logical groupings on each individual chromosome—albeit not quite as successfully as if your parents have tested.

Academic or Statistical Phasing

How can scientists phase your DNA if neither of your parents have tested?

DNA often "travels together" in groups, just like our ancestors did. Scientists have discovered that at specific addresses, the neighbor DNA is most likely to be particular nucleotides.

Pairwise bonding is the process used for preparing your DNA to identify your populations of origin by reassembling your DNA into two strands—one from Mom and one from Dad.

Looking at your raw data DNA results, we see that location #1 is an A. Next, we notice that the A has bonded with an T to make a pair. Your nucleotide values at this location are AT.

	#1	#2	#3	#4	#5	#6	#7	#8	#9	#10
Blue People - 90%	A	A	A	A	A	A	A	A	A	A
Mom	A									
Dad	T									

Of course, if one parent has tested, filling in the blanks is easy.

But if neither parent has tested, the vendor uses two pieces of knowledge:

- The knowledge of most common choices for neighbor addresses in human DNA
- The knowledge of the most common choices at those locations in each population tested

Let's say that you have another AT, but we don't know whether the T or the A comes from your mother.

	#1	#2	#3	#4	#5	#6	#7	#8	#9	#10
Blue People - 90%	A	A	A	A	A	A	A	A	A	A
Mom	A	A								
Dad	T	T								

In location 1, an A is the most common neighbor for A. Also, T is the most common neighbor for T at this location. Therefore, each location is reassembled by sorting your two values at each location into strands that, if correct, will eventually represent your mother and father. In other words, in this example, A is placed with A and T with T on the same "side."

Each chromosome is "reassembled" individually and independently, so your mother's "side" on one chromosome could be your father's side on a different chromosome. The vendors can't determine who is who without at least one parent testing, and not all vendors use parents to check their statistical or academic phasing results.

Even if your parents have tested, depending on the vendor, your DNA will likely be tentatively "phased" using this academic or statistical phasing methodology, then corrected using parental phasing. Statistical or academic phasing is not foolproof, but it's better than nothing when there are no parents to test. It actually performs amazingly well.

Imputation

There's another method used to infer DNA in some regions where it may be missing. You may have transferred a DNA file from one vendor to another. Vendors don't always test the exact same locations of DNA, so the "blanks" in the DNA somehow need to be filled in for the best ethnicity and matching results.

	#1	#2	#3	#4	#5	#6	#7	#8	#9	#10
Blue People - 90%	A	A	A	A	A	A	A	A	A	A
Mom	A	A				A	A	A	A	A
Dad	T	T				C	C	C	C	C

In the above case, you can phase your DNA in every location except for 3, 4, and 5. The vendor this person transferred from didn't test those locations, so the vendor you transferred to needs to figure out what would reasonably be found in those locations in order to produce Ethnicity Estimates and reliable matching.

Understanding pairwise bonding and common neighbor choices for DNA in specific populations, the vendor can infer the following:

- When A's are found in locations 1–2 and 6–10, A's are normally also found at locations 3–5.

- In the Blue Finnish People population, A's are found in locations 1–10 90% of the time.

- When T's are found in locations 1–2 and C's are found in locations 6–10, typically T's are found in locations 3–5.

- In the Pink People population, TTTTTCCCCC is found at locations 1–10 80% of the time.

	#1	#2	#3	#4	#5	#6	#7	#8	#9	#10
Blue People - 90%	A	A	A	A	A	A	A	A	A	A
Mom	A	A	A	A	A	A	A	A	A	A
Dad	T	T	T	T	T	C	C	C	C	C
Pink People - 80%	T	T	T	T	T	C	C	C	C	C

Not all vendors adjust a tester's ethnicity results based on parental phasing.

When using ethnicity results in combination with matching, looking for relatives who share the same ethnicity on the same segments becomes important for tracking Native segments back in time to the proper ancestor.

Ethnicity Results

Ethnicity results are only educated scientific estimates.[68] Seriously! They can be wrong in either direction, meaning omitting an ethnicity, population, or region that is present in a person's genealogy, or including some that are not.[69] Now that you understand how closely the Blue Finnish People are genetically linked to their neighbors, and how DNA is inherited, you can understand why.

Typically, the smaller the percentage, the more likely it is to be incorrect—but that's not always true by any means. Ethnicity or population results are the most accurate at the continental level, as well as for Native American and Jewish people:

- Europe
- Asia
- Africa
- Native American
- Jewish

Ethnicity results are reported by vendors in various, proprietary ways based on a compilation of publicly available research reference panels combined with their own customers. Of course, genealogists want more specificity than continents, so companies strive to find commonalities and differences among populations in countries or regions.

---

[68] https://dna-explained.com/2018/12/28/ethnicity-is-just-an-estimate-yes-really/
[69] https://dna-explained.com/2016/02/10/ethnicity-testing-a-conundrum/

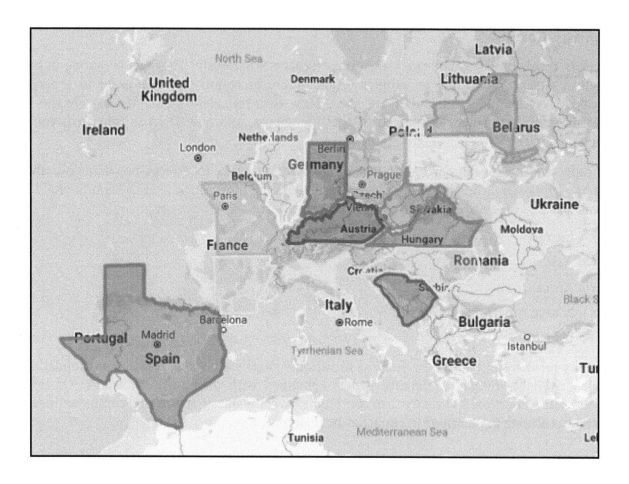

Keep in mind that what we are asking testing companies to do is to determine genetic differences in areas the size of individual states in the United States.[70] Europe is more alike than different.[71]

Each vendor has its own databases and its own internal science team that creates algorithms to determine your ethnicity and population results. Some vendors layer additional features and tools on top of ethnicity results.

In Part 3 we'll see what the major four vendors have to offer in terms of ethnicity and related features that are relevant to our search for Native American ancestors.

---

[70] https://dna-explained.com/2019/11/20/making-sense-of-ethnicity-updates/
[71] https://en.wikipedia.org/wiki/Genetic_history_of_Europe

Geography and Native American Ethnicity

People whose ethnicity results point to Native American heritage often find both North and South America included. Some people also find Northwest Asia, meaning Siberia. Southern Asia, Central Asia, and other Asian regions are not considered to be indicative of Native heritage. Conversely, I've never seen anyone who is confirmed to have Native ancestry have results that show only Siberian ethnicity without North or South American ethnicity too.

Remember, Native people had no one other than other Native people who arrived in small migratory groups with whom to intermarry for thousands of years, so Native people in North and South America are more alike than different. They share the same small population of ancestors.

I co-administer the American Indian Project at FamilyTreeDNA as a volunteer and am involved with several other tribal and haplogroup projects. These projects provide me with the opportunity to evaluate the DNA results of many project members.

I have noticed that people who belong to West Coast tribes, specifically tribes and peoples along the Alaskan/Canadian/US Pacific coastline islands, tend to carry higher percentages of Siberian or Northwest Asian DNA than Native people further inland. Siberian results are in addition to Native American results.

Rarely, a West Coast Native person shows a small percentage of Polynesian DNA. Some mainland Native people intermarried with Native Hawaiians in the 1800s,[72] endowing their descendants with both Polynesian and Native DNA today. Hawaiian men were seamen, whalers, and laborers on ships[73] beginning in 1811. Remnants of their DNA are sometimes found today in the Pacific Northwest.[74]

For years, potential small amounts of Polynesian admixture (other than the known mariner interaction mentioned above), either from Hawaii or other Pacific islands, have been discussed and debated. We know that if that admixture did occur, it isn't recent because those genetic signatures are not dominantly found. If Polynesian admixture does exist, it would be a background or ghost signal found only in regional, probably South American, coastal populations. It's possible that one or two isolated contacts occurred, perhaps Kon-Tiki style boats that landed and never returned.

In June of 2020, a surprising article was published confirming that sometime between 700 and 1,000 years ago, at least one contact was made between Native people currently found in Colombia and the South Pacific islands.[75] This proof exists in both a background Native signal that matches most closely with Native people from Colombia and in sweet potatoes, also native to South America. Of course, if pollination went in one direction, it could also have gone in the other direction, with a few Polynesian men landing in South America as well.

---

[72] https://www.civilbeat.org/2020/05/tracing-californias-lost-tribe-of-hawaiians/
[73] https://www.nps.gov/articles/hawaiiansatfortvancouver.htm
[74] https://core.ac.uk/download/pdf/5014697.pdf; https://www.familytreedna.com/groups/hawaiiansofthe-pacific-northwest/about
[75] https://www.nature.com/articles/d41586-020-01983-5

In June of 2021, Willerslev and Meltzer published "Peopling of the Americas as inferred from ancient genomics,"[76] in which they provide an excellent summary of current knowledge. They mention that early Polynesian admixture in South America, in the 1300s or before, is possible, but not established. Easter Islanders show small amounts of Native American admixture, which has yet to be explained.

The jury is still out on this topic, but I can't help but wonder if mitochondrial DNA haplogroup F1a1a might provide a clue.

---

[76] https://www.nature.com/articles/s41586-021-03499-y

PART 3:
DNA TESTING VENDORS AND AUTOSOMAL TOOLS

Vendors Rearrange the Furniture from Time to Time

Each vendor makes changes and improvements in its features and website design from time to time. I've included detailed step-by-step instructions in this book, but eventually, the vendors will change something. The feature might be moved to a place that makes more sense, colors and icons might be updated, or new functionality added.

Most of the time, vendors don't remove features, just rearrange the furniture a bit. I cover major changes on my blog at www.dnaexplain.com. You can always search the vendor's help center or reach out via email, phone, or chat to contact the vendor as well.

FamilyTreeDNA

FamilyTreeDNA's autosomal DNA test is called Family Finder. FamilyTreeDNA is the only one of the big four testing companies that offers multiple types of DNA testing. In addition to autosomal testing, customers can also order Y and mitochondrial DNA tests independently from autosomal. We will review those in separate sections.

FamilyTreeDNA myOrigins

The dashboard on each tester's personal page is divided into sections. The Autosomal DNA Results & Tools section shows the various tools available.

Ethnicity tools to assist with Native American genealogy can be found under the myOrigins and Chromosome Painting tabs. Let's start with myOrigins.

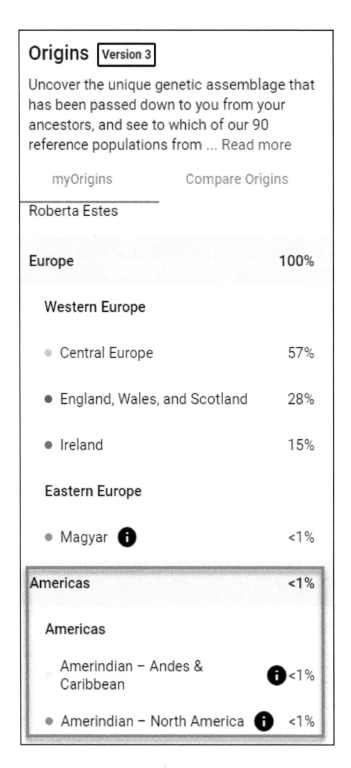

Each vendor, at some location on its pages, will tell you how many worldwide reference populations it is using for comparison.

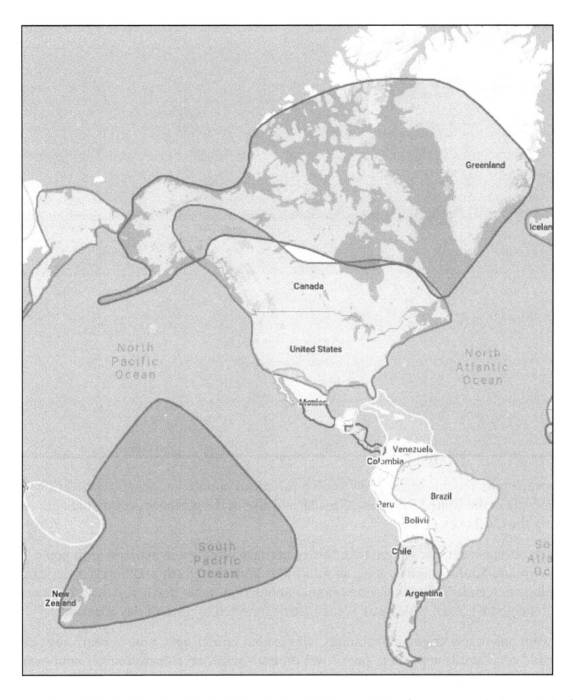

Currently, in myOrigins Version 3 (V3), FamilyTreeDNA uses 90 reference populations, including nine Native American regions, but future versions will change.

Each population is shown on an associated map for each tester.

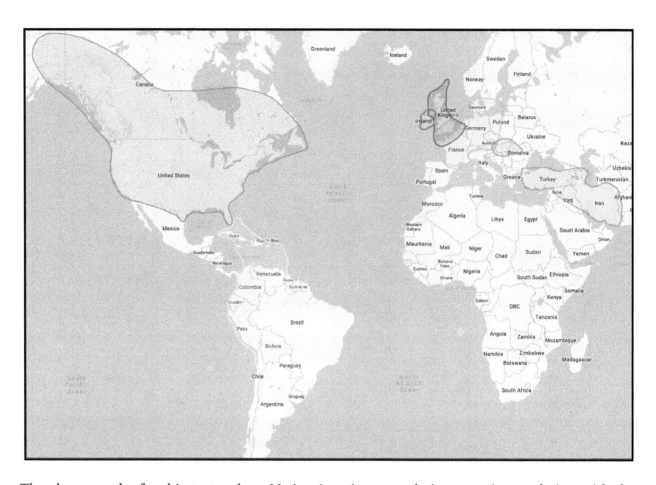

The above results for this tester show Native American population genetic correlation with the Native people in the United States and Canada, and also in the northern portion of South America, including the Caribbean.

It's worth noting again that people with Native heritage often show matches with populations in both North and South America. Keep in mind that both the North and South American Native populations descended from the same original population in far northwest Asia before crossing now-submerged Beringia, which was at that time connected to present-day Alaska.

There were only a few original inhabitants who settled on Beringia, now beneath the sea.[77] This small band of migrants appears to have lived on Beringia, then sometime later continued on to settle what would become the American continents. There is still speculation about how many migrations occurred, but we know there were at least two, plus some back-migration as well. Eventually—11,000 years ago—seawater covered Beringia, and the people who had crossed into the Americas populated both continents.

---

[77] https://en.wikipedia.org/wiki/Beringia

FamilyTreeDNA myOrigins Match Comparisons

A second myOrigins option is Compare Origins, which allows you to compare your ethnicity categories with those of your matches. When searching for an ethnicity where you carry a small percentage, this comparison allows you to focus on people who also carry that same ethnicity.[78]

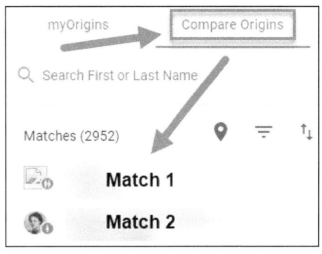

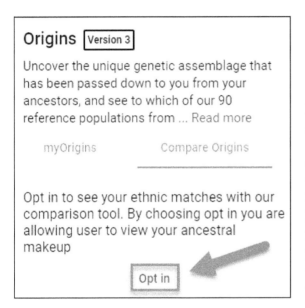

If you have not opted in for ethnicity comparison with others, you'll be prompted to do so.

After opting in, you'll be able to compare your ethnicity with other matches who have also opted in. They will be able to view your ethnicity too. Please note that you will have matches who have not opted in, and you will not see their names in your list of matches on this page. Testers cannot assume that just because someone is absent from this list, they don't have a specific ethnicity.

The tiny icons beside the picture of your match will indicate which side of your family this match is from, assuming you've linked your matches to the proper relative in your tree,[79] and assuming that the match can be assigned to one side or the other based on your linked matches.

The top female icon indicates your mother's side and the bottom male your father's side; the middle icon with two figures indicates someone who is related to you through both sides, such as a full sibling or one of your children or nieces/nephews.

Click on the match to see the comparison.

[78] https://dna-explained.com/2020/11/12/dna-tidbit-2-familytreednas-compare-origins-map/

[79] https://dna-explained.com/2019/11/06/triangulation-in-action-at-family-tree-dna/

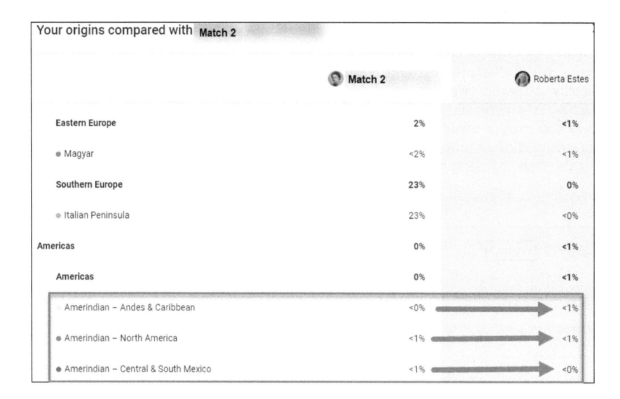

In this case, Match 2 and the tester both have Native regions. This doesn't mean that two people necessarily match on the same segment of DNA, or that they even match on any Native segment of DNA. It only means that they are each reported to have a small amount of Native heritage. This may or may not be relevant to your match with this person.

When might this match be important? It could be important if you want to determine which side of your family your Native heritage came from.

Even if you have a small amount of Native DNA, you should match one of your two parents, meaning your parent should carry that ethnicity on the same DNA segment.

Ethnicity can also be identical by chance, meaning not by descent, so parental phasing helps immensely.

FamilyTreeDNA Matrilineal and Patrilineal Pins

A third feature of the myOrigins map that you may find useful is the ability to enable or disable Y DNA and mitochondrial DNA ancestral pins on the map. The purpose is to see if any of your matches have a direct line ancestor that is Native American. That ancestor may or may not be related to you, but it's another piece of information.

On the Compare Origins page, you'll see a balloon pin beside your match total.

Clicking on this pin allows you to activate all the pins of the locations of your matches' earliest known paternal (Y) or maternal (mtDNA) ancestors.

Map

☐ Show All Paternal Ancestor Markers

☐ Show All Maternal Ancestor Markers

What FamilyTreeDNA is really asking customers for are patrilineal and matrilineal ancestors who represent the earliest known ancestors of the testers' Y DNA and mitochondrial DNA lines, but that isn't always what people enter. I've seen many males listed as the earliest known direct "maternal" ancestor, which can't be accurate, of course, for mitochondrial DNA. If you're interested in following up, you can view your match's profile on your match list.

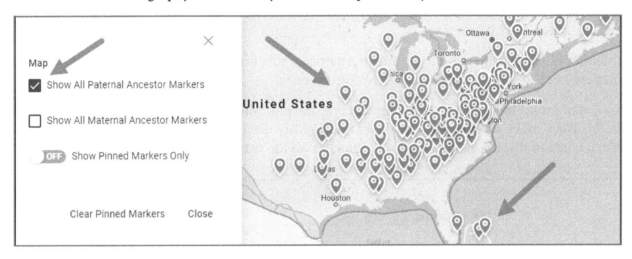

In this example, I've selected my matches that have direct paternal ancestor pins on the map. These United States pins may indicate Native American ancestors, or they may simply indicate someone who is "brickwalled" in the United States. It's easy to check for all Native American haplogroups by sorting or scanning that column on your downloaded matches CSV file.

Just because someone shows a pin doesn't mean they have taken a Y or mitochondrial DNA test. It simply means they've entered the names of their earliest known ancestors, along with the geographic coordinates. If you click on their pin, you can view their ancestor information, along with their haplogroup information if they have taken a Y or mitochondrial DNA test. The haplogroup information will reveal if those linear ancestors are Native or not.

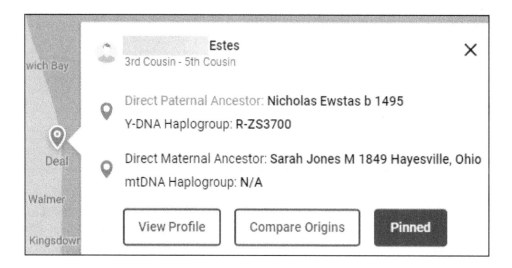

In this case, the Estes match's Y DNA is Y haplogroup R, which is not Native. The match has not taken the mtDNA test, so the haplogroup is noted as N/A, which means "not applicable." N/A does not mean Native American.

If neither of these haplogroups are Native American, this immediately tells you that these direct lines are not the source of this match's Native ancestry.

If you don't want to view the entire map, but only the pins for a specific match or multiple matches on this page, make sure the pins for the entire page are disabled, then click on the pin beside the match name to display the pins for those matches on the map.

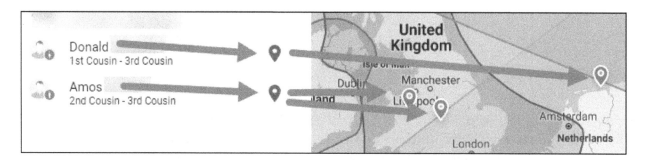

In this case, Donald has only tested and entered information for his Y DNA, while Amos has tested and entered geographic information for both Y and mitochondrial DNA.

FamilyTreeDNA myOrigins Chromosome Painting

FamilyTreeDNA provides population-based chromosome painting.

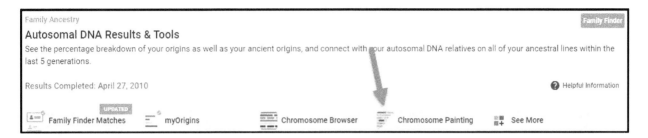

This tool is particularly useful when mapping ancestors to specific segments of DNA.

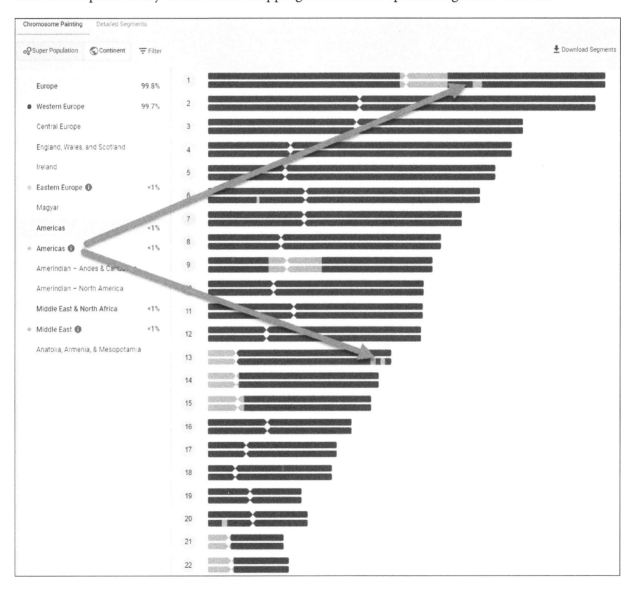

At the top of the page, testers can choose to display either Super Populations or Continents.

Each population/continent is mapped to a particular portion of a chromosome. Both of your chromosomes are displayed, one from your mother and one from your father—but vendors can't always tell which population or ethnicity should be attributed to each parent. Therefore, the top

45

and bottom chromosome cannot always be interpreted to be mother and father, especially not on different chromosomes.

Said another way, on chromosome 1, or even portions of chromosome 1, mother may be the top chromosome and father the bottom one. On chromosome 2, the reverse may be true. The only way to assure proper distribution of populations on your chromosomes is as follows:

- Test either or both parents and compare your results.
- Vendors could then adjust your chromosome painting based on the DNA of your parents, although that sometimes doesn't work flawlessly either.

It's unclear whether all vendors adjust results when parents have tested.

Remember that your DNA can combine in ways that cause matches to incorrect populations, especially in the case of trace amounts where less matching DNA is required for a population match.

You can view the actual locations of your population segments by selecting the Detailed Segments tab at the top of the page. By selecting this, you can view the addresses of the segments that are attributed to specific populations, either Super Populations or Continents.[80]

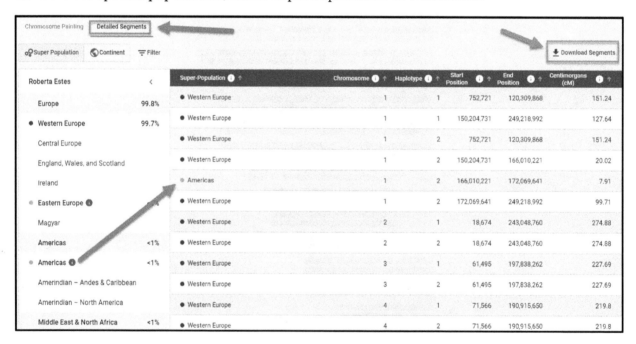

You can also choose the Download Segments button in the top right-hand corner for use when evaluating your matches or to use with third-party tools like DNAPainter.[81]

---

[80] https://blog.familytreedna.com/wp-content/uploads/2021/08/myOrigins_3_WhitePaper.pdf
[81] https://dna-explained.com/2021/09/01/familytreednas-chromosome-painting-just-arrived/

MyHeritage

MyHeritage Ethnicity

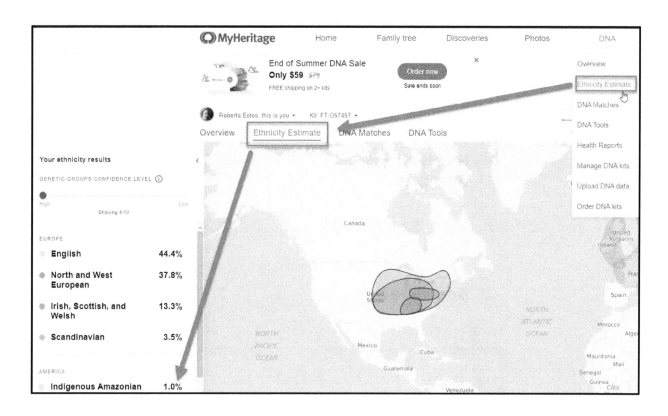

MyHeritage provides two ethnicity tools, both shown under your DNA Ethnicity Estimate:

- Percentage of 42 ethnicities

- Match clusters within 2,114 Genetic Groups[82]

---

[82] https://dna-explained.com/2020/12/24/introducing-genetic-groups-at-myheritage/

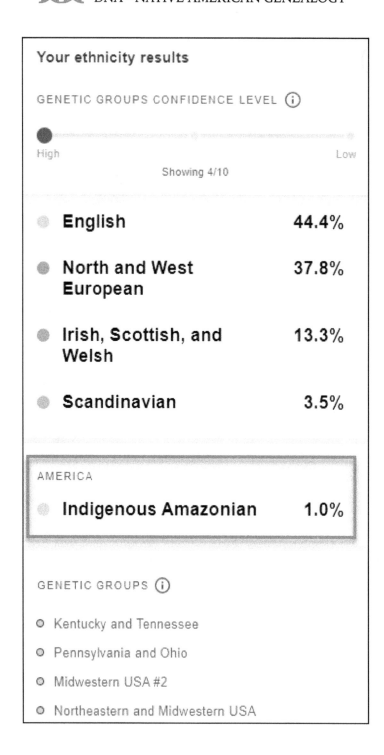

At MyHeritage, your ethnicity percentages are displayed in colored regions, and your Genetic Groups are displayed with dark bands around the group.

MyHeritage Genetic Groups

Genetic Groups are locations where groups of people match you, overlayed on your ethnicity map.

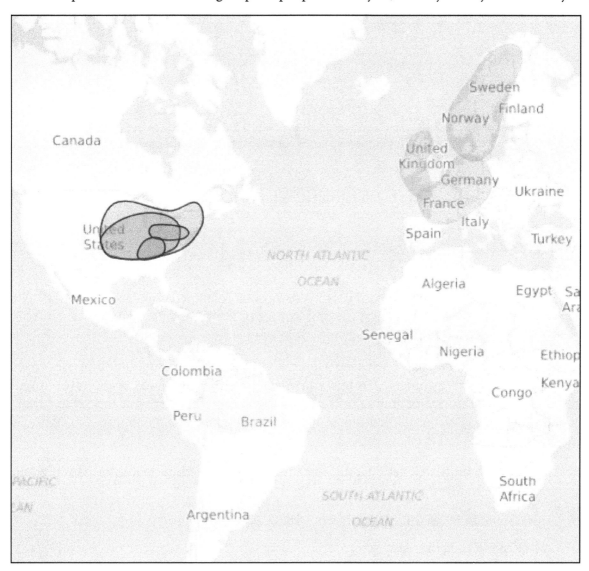

The Genetic Groups confidence bar near the top of the page displays groups that are formed based on confidence levels.

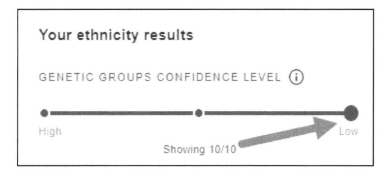

Using the confidence bar in the graphic, only the 4 Genetic Groups with the highest confidence level are shown when the bar is at the highest level, to the far left. By sliding the bar to the far right, at the lowest confidence level, all 10 Genetic Groups will be shown on the map.

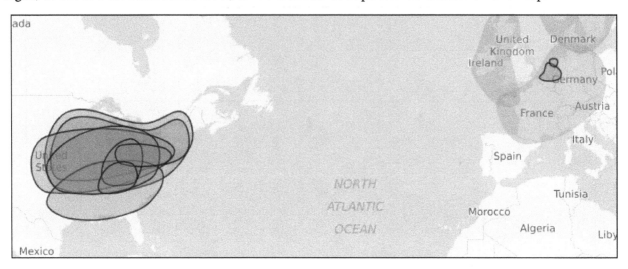

While ethnicity is based solely on comparisons to various reference populations, Genetic Groups are formed when you match the DNA of some subset of MyHeritage's customer base who show ancestors from particular populations or regions in their trees.

In my case, you can see that I have no Genetic Groups that appear superimposed over my Indigenous Amazonian ethnicity. Groups can form in either original locations or migration destinations. The ethnicity of immigrants would appear in their original home location. For example, in the areas of the United States where my Genetic Groups appear, Germans, Swiss, English, Welch, and Scots-Irish all settled.

The tester can click on the Genetic Group, which then reveals additional information about the group, such as the following:

- Time frame in 50-year increments from 1600–2000

- Places mentioned in trees

- Common surnames

- Common given names

- Common ethnicities

- Related groups

By selecting a Genetic Group, a heat map is then displayed that shows migration patterns for that Genetic Group—in other words, where people in that Genetic Group, and their descendants, can be found at various points in history.

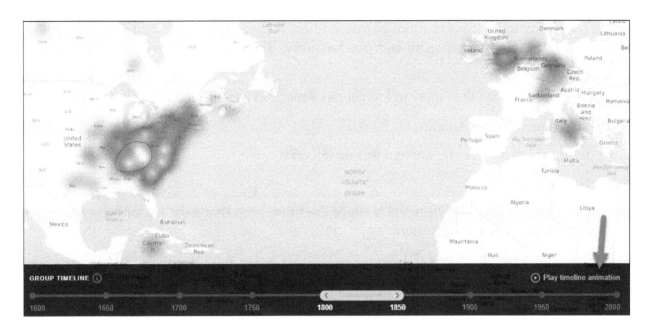

This is my Kentucky and Tennessee group from 1800–1850. The migration pattern is clear. Ancestor populations found in that location originated in specific regions in Europe, first settled in the Atlantic shore regions, then began migrating to the next frontiers further south and west. Be sure to play the timeline animation.

MyHeritage has the added benefit of being able to filter matches by ethnicity and by Genetic Groups, allowing customers to select one of each in any combination.[83] Note that the names of the ethnicities aren't the same and don't exactly overlap.

For example, Indigenous Amazonian located between Colombia and Brazil only slightly overlaps the Mesoamerican and Andean category, shown below.

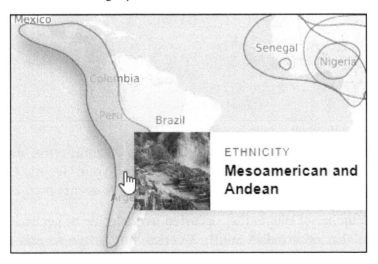

---

[83] https://dna-explained.com/2021/06/04/new-genetic-groups-filter-at-myheritage/

Having the ability to use combinations of match filters is powerful. For example, you could filter for both Native American ethnicity and the Kentucky, Tennessee, Virginia, and Ohio Genetic Group.

Ethnicity filter selections that apply to Indigenous American heritage include the following:

- Mesoamerican and Andean

- Inuit, which includes far Eastern Russia (Siberia)

- Native American

Sharing some percentage of indigenous heritage does not mean that's the reason why you match another tester, but it is a place to start.

It's also possible that a person's indigenous results are either false positives or false negatives, especially if either person is only showing small percentages.

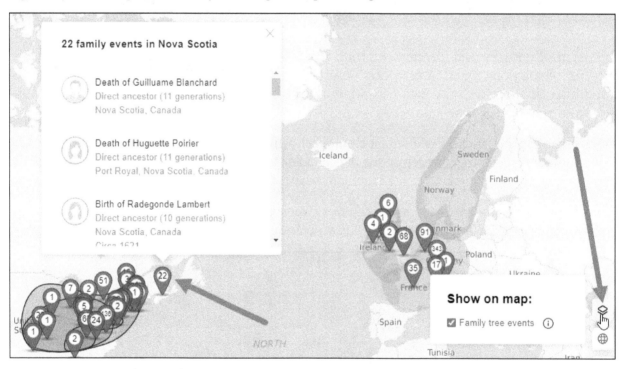

Selecting the drop-down diamond at far-right shows "Family tree events" on the map, superimposed on top of both your Ethnicity Estimate and your Genetic Groups. This ties the ancestors in your tree to the places where their significant life events occurred.

Each pin shows the number of events that occurred in a specific or general location. In my case, there were no events that occurred in South America, but I have several ancestors from Nova Scotia, one source of my Native American heritage, even though that region is not shown in my Ethnicity Estimate or Genetic Groups.

MyHeritage Shared Ethnicity

MyHeritage provides ethnicity filters for DNA matches.

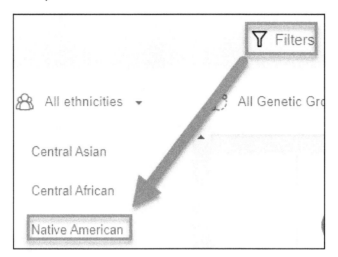

After selecting this filter, only your matches with the specific ethnicity you've selected will be shown. Review each match to see your compared ethnicity.

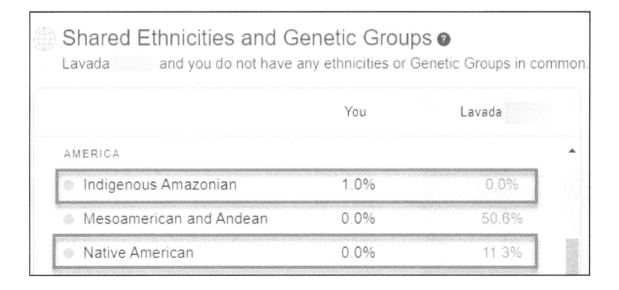

Ancestry

Ancestry and Ethnicity

Ethnicity at Ancestry is found in your DNA Story.

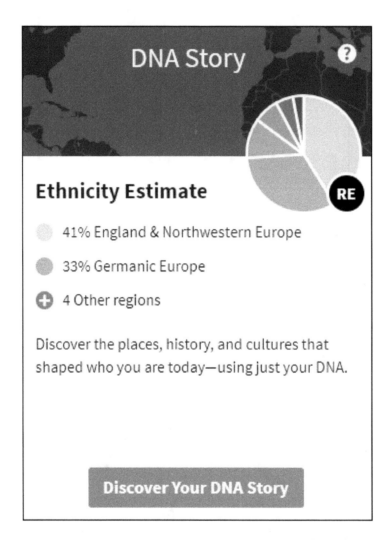

Ancestry provides ethnicity percentages for more than 1,400 regions and DNA Genetic Communities. Ancestry states that communities are much smaller than ethnicity regions and only reach back 50–300 years, while ethnicity reaches further back in time.

Ethnicity Estimate   🔗 Share

England & Northwestern Europe	41% >
Germanic Europe	33% >
Ireland	11% >
France	7% >
Wales	5% >
Norway	3% >

Additional Communities

Lower Midwest & Virginia Settlers >
From your regions: England & Northwestern Europe

10 Possible Ancestor Stories Found

   Missouri Ozarks & East Tennessee Settlers

Pennsylvania, Ohio & Indiana Settlers >
From your regions: England & Northwestern Europe; Germanic Eur...

8 Possible Ancestor Stories Found

   Alleghenies & Northeast Indiana Settlers

See other regions tested   1,100+

In addition to providing an Ethnicity Estimate, Ancestry provides testers with information about Additional Communities[84] in which their matches' ancestors are found.

---

[84] https://dna-explained.com/2020/11/18/dna-tidbit-3-ancestrys-genetic-communities/

Ancestry Genetic Communities

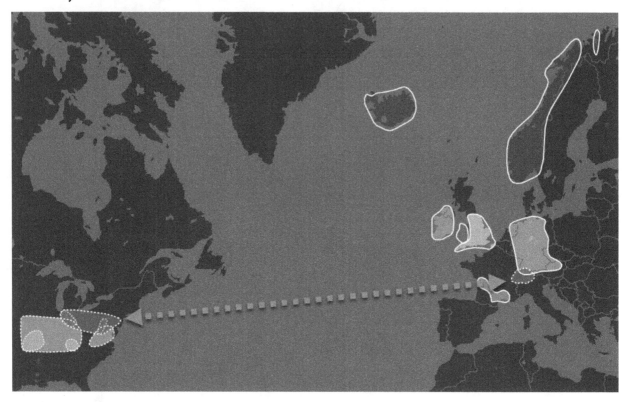

At Ancestry, Ethnicity Estimates are shown with solid lines surrounding regions of color and Genetic Communities are shown with hashed lines. Note that migration is shown by the same color and hash pattern appearing in multiple parts of the globe.

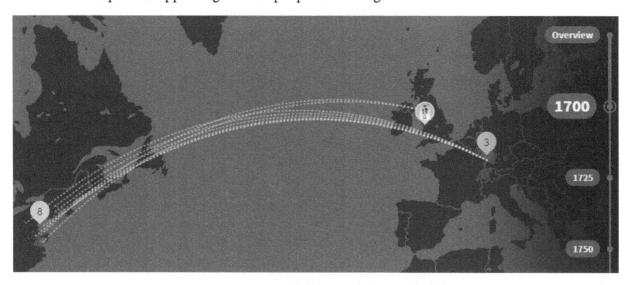

By clicking on one of your Genetic Communities, and then an associated timeline, a pin will appear with the number of ancestors within the marked area during that time. For example, in 1700 I had three ancestors in Switzerland and Germany.

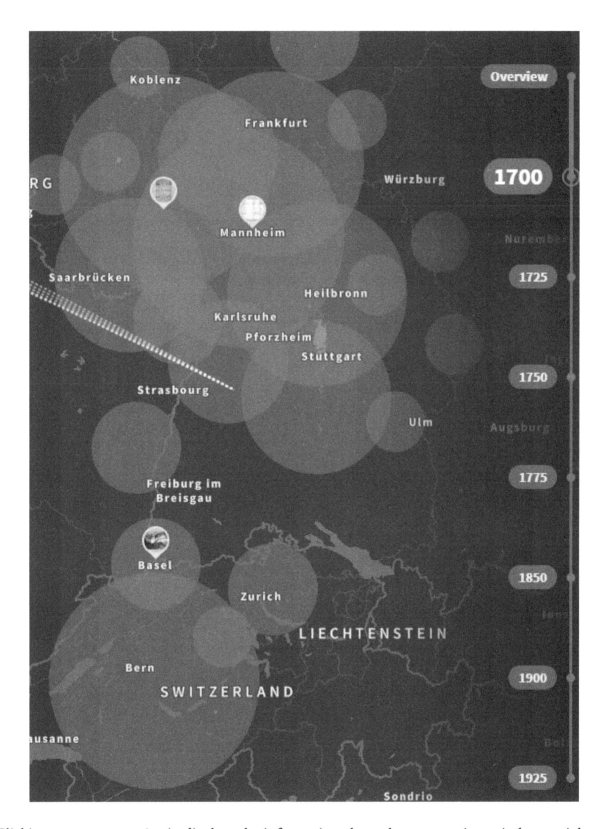

Clicking on an ancestor's pin displays the information about the ancestor in a window at right.

Note that *only* ancestors who fall within that *particular* Genetic Community are shown, not ancestors who fall within an Ethnicity Estimate region or in a different Genetic Community.

In the Americas, with the widespread history of European settlement, it's nearly impossible to determine if finding an ancestor in a specific Genetic Community is reflective of indigenous or immigrant ancestors, or both.

America

- **Indigenous Americas—Andean**
  11 regions

- **Indigenous Americas—Central**
  9 regions

- **Indigenous Americas—Colombia & Venezuela**
  11 regions

- **Indigenous Americas—Mexico**
  87 regions

- **Indigenous Americas—North**

- **Indigenous Americas—Yucatan Peninsula**

- **Indigenous Arctic**

- **Indigenous Cuba**

- **Indigenous Eastern South America**
  1 region

- **Indigenous Haiti & Dominican Republic**

- **Indigenous Puerto Rico**

- **Additional South American Communities**
  2 regions

Ancestry reports on several Native geographic regions between both Ethnicity Estimates and Genetic Communities.

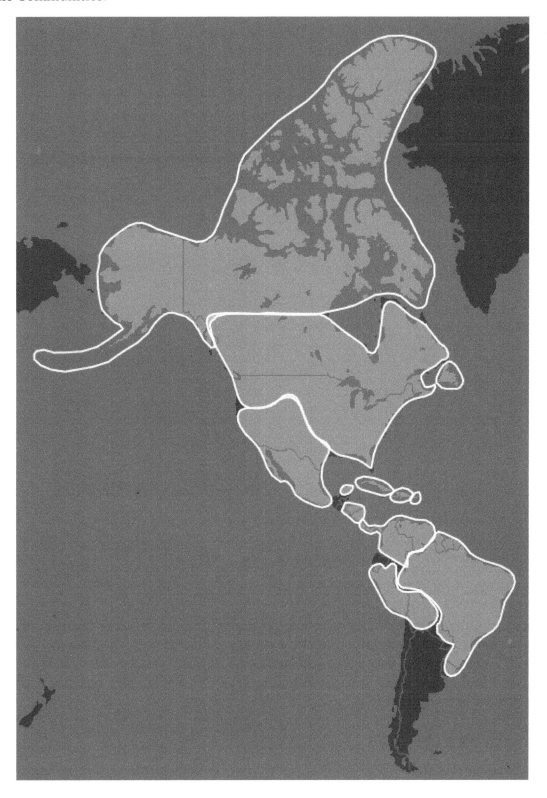

Ancestry showed no Native genetic heritage for my results, although FamilyTreeDNA, 23andMe, and MyHeritage all do. Furthermore, some of the Native segments identified by both 23andMe and FamilyTreeDNA correspond and can be traced to ancestors whose Native heritage can be confirmed using genealogical records, Y DNA, mitochondrial DNA, and autosomal segment matching to descendants.

Ancestry Shared Ethnicity

By reviewing each match at Ancestry, you can compare your shared ethnicity percentages.

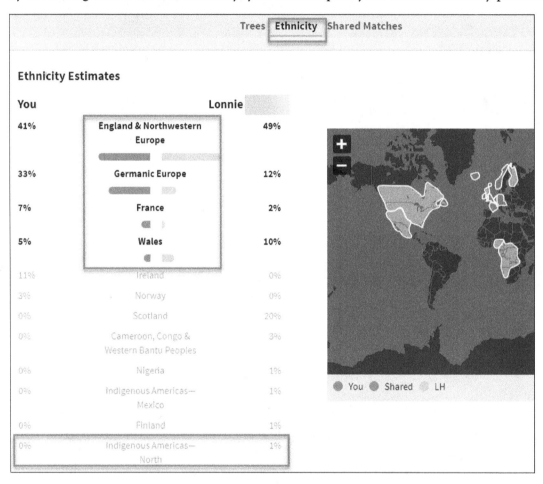

Unfortunately, unlike the other vendors, Ancestry doesn't offer chromosome segment information nor chromosome ethnicity painting, so you have no way to determine if you share the same Native segment, or if you and other matches triangulate. Some Ancestry testers download their raw data file and tree,[85] and upload them to either FamilyTreeDNA or MyHeritage, or both, to obtain the benefits at those organizations.[86]

---

[85] https://dna-explained.com/2020/06/30/download-your-ancestry-tree-and-upload-it-elsewhere-for-added-benefit/
[86] https://dna-explained.com/2019/11/04/dna-file-upload-download-and-transfer-instructions-to-and-from-dna-testing-companies/

23andMe

23andMe Ancestry Composition

23andMe is somewhat different than the other companies, given that it doesn't support genealogical family trees created by testers in genealogical software. It does create a pseudo-genetic tree, attempting to position your closest matches in their proper location in a tree based on the amount of DNA shared between you and your matches, and how your matches match with each other.

Users can enter their ancestors' names for the past four generations to personalize the experience and can correct a predicted relationship. While this tree is helpful in terms of positioning close matches, it's not directly useful for the identification of Native ancestors. It can, however, be useful by allowing you to view the haplogroups of matches positioned in your tree to see if the haplogroups are of Native origin.

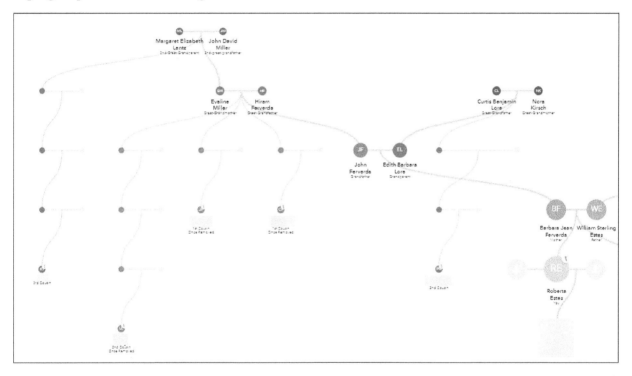

These estimated positions are often not precisely correct, but unless a match is related on both sides of your tree, they will be positioned generally accurately, at least as far as maternally or paternally is concerned. Don't assume this system-generated tree is correct without confirmation, though having even an approximate genetic tree to work with is an important tool in its own right.

23andMe is best known for its accurate ethnicity results called Ancestry Composition, found under the Ancestry tab at the top. Of course, no vendor is accurate 100% of the time, and as you compare my results that I've used for illustrations, you can see the wide variance among vendors.

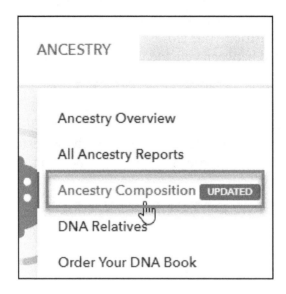

At 23andMe, Ancestry Composition ethnicity estimates use 45 reference populations.

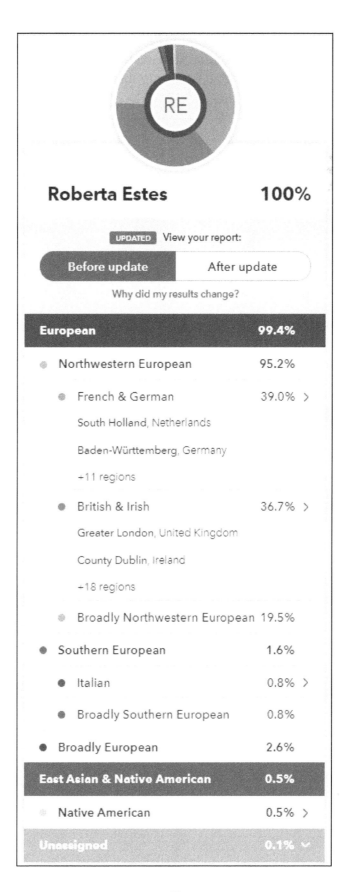

23andMe periodically updates Ancestry Composition ethnicity results, as do the rest of the vendors. Unfortunately, it no longer paints small percentages on the map. As you can see below, my Native results are missing. Pay attention to the numbers, not the map, especially when dealing with trace amounts of DNA.

Recently, 23andMe added eight regions within the United States and southern Canada based on the grandparents of testers, but its blog states that only about 10% of its customers with Native Heritage receive one of these regions.[87] Most customers remain more broadly Native.

The 23andMe Native American regions are as follows:

- Alaska, which includes some portion of western Canada

- Columbia River Basin, which includes Washington, part of southwest Canada, Idaho, and Oregon

- Great Basin and Colorado River Basin, which includes Nevada, California, part of southern Idaho, and Arizona

- Great Lakes and Canada, which includes the upper Midwest, Michigan, Wisconsin, Minnesota, parts of North Dakota, Montana, Oklahoma, Indiana, Illinois, Kansas, and central and southern Canada

- Northeast, which includes New York, Vermont, New Hampshire, Massachusetts, Connecticut, New Jersey, Rhode Island, and Maine, along with parts of Indiana, Michigan, Pennsylvania, Ohio, and Oklahoma

- Plains, which includes South Dakota, parts of Oklahoma, North Dakota, Montana, southern Minnesota, and Nebraska

- South Central, which includes Oklahoma, parts of Missouri, Arkansas, Kansas, Texas, Louisiana, Alabama, the Florida Panhandle, and Mississippi

- Southwest, which includes New Mexico, parts of Oklahoma, Utah, Colorado, and Arizona

You may be wondering why the Northeast group includes Oklahoma. Remember that many tribes, including the Delaware who formerly lived in New Jersey, were displaced initially into Kansas, then settled in Oklahoma in 1867.[88]

You may notice a section called "Recent Ancestry in the Americas" under the Ancestry Composition, Scientific Details tab. 23andMe states that Ancestry Compositions are considered to be "Old World" populations, before populations were highly admixed. In regions like Puerto Rico—where much of the population reflects a combination of Native American, African, and European populations that have intermixed in the past 500 years—23andMe may classify your results as "Recent Ancestry in the Americas." I'm not clear about the difference between that classification and the "Native American" categories because there are few individuals in the Native population today who are not admixed with people from groups who arrived in the past 500 years.

---

[87] https://blog.23andme.com/ancestry-reports/indigenous-genetic-ancestry/
[88] https://www.okhistory.org/publications/enc/entry.php?entry=DE011

23andMe Ancestry Timeline

23andMe provides an Ancestry Timeline under the Ancestry Composition tab, but care needs to be taken with the interpretation of these results.[89]

Any population category does not, or may not, descend from solely one ancestor. In other words, I don't have one British/Irish ancestor who lived in the early 1900s, but I have many British/Irish ancestors whose DNA, combined, created enough in total to appear to be one person who lived in the early 1900s.

This is the result of one or more[90] of the following:

- Multiple ancestors who share the same origins
- Pedigree collapse, where you descend from individual ancestors more than once
- Endogamy

I have multiple Native American ancestors on both of my parents' sides.

My Ancestry Composition results have shifted over time, and now both French and German as well as British and Irish have shifted to 1930, and my Native American category has disappeared altogether, along with both Scandinavian and Eastern Europe. Somehow, inexplicably, I've picked up Italian, which looks to replace Eastern Europe and remains a mystery unsupported by decades of genealogical research.

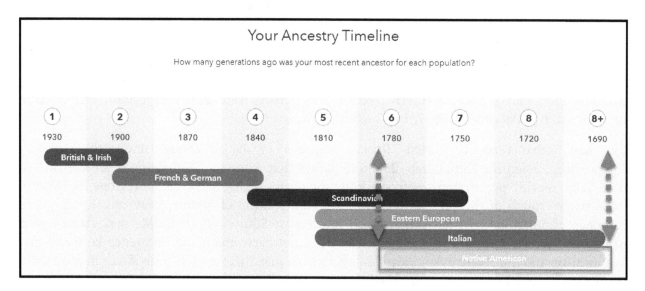

One thing about Ethnicity Estimates—if you don't like them, just sit tight as they will change over time. This is the perfect example of why they are called estimates.

---

[89] https://permalinks.23andme.com/pdf/23-14_admixture_date_estimator.pdf
[90] https://dna-explained.com/2021/07/23/whats-the-difference-between-pedigree-collapse-and-endogamy/

None of my ancestors were living anywhere other than in the United States by 1930. No one was living in France, Germany, Great Britain, or Ireland. My last ancestor born overseas was born in 1854 in the Netherlands. All my British and Irish ancestors were in America before 1762, when my last English ancestor to leave England was born in London. My last German ancestor to leave was born in Germany in 1841. My last French ancestor was born in France before the Acadian settlement in Nova Scotia beginning in 1605.[91]

In other words, my "total" amount of a specific ethnicity or population, British/Irish for example, might be equal to one ancestor who was born in Britain or Ireland in 1930, but those pieces are made up on the "English/Irish" DNA segments of multiple ancestors who lived far back in time on both sides of my tree.

Do not interpret this timeline literally, and do not rely on this information for genealogy.

23andMe Match Comparisons

23andMe also provides a feature to compare ethnicity results of testers with their parents if at least one parent has tested, although small amounts are not reported accurately.

In the example below, the child shows a trace amount of Native American ancestry.

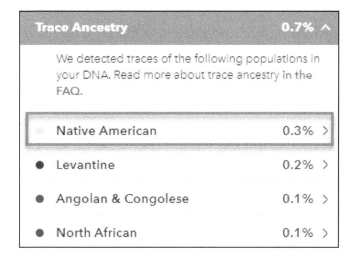

However, when the child's results are compared to the parent's in their Parental Inheritance Report, their Native results are not properly reported.

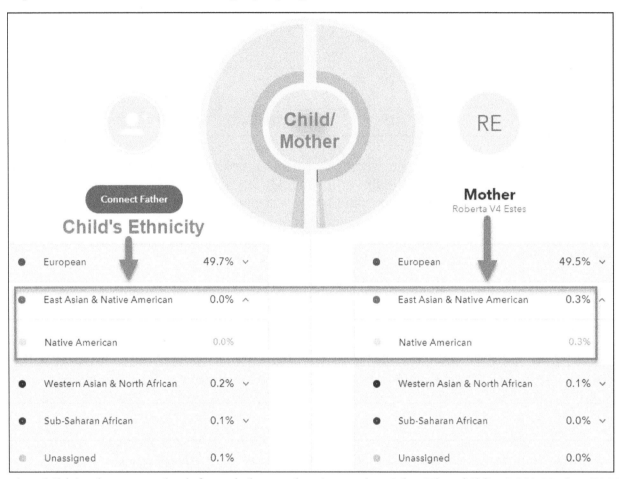

The child is shown on the left, and the mother is on the right. The child's 0.3% Native DNA doesn't show in this display, but it does in their totals.

If both parents have tested, the father's overlapping ethnicity with the child would be shown on the left side of the circle. Since only one parent tested, the overlapping portions of the regions selected are shown on the right portion of the circle.

Fortunately, you can see for yourself if this section of your results make sense and is accurate.

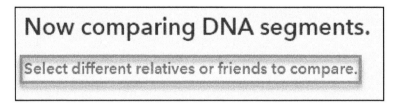

You can also select other matches and compare your ethnicity results, side by side, by clicking on any match and scrolling down to Compare your Ancestry.

Compare your Ancestry

Compare your genetic ancestries to discover your shared origins and unique family histories.

Ancestry Composition

Compare your DNA connections to populations around the world.

You		S:	
See full report		See full report	
99.5%	● European	99.0%	⌄
0.0%	● Western Asian & North African	0.9%	⌄
0.3%	● East Asian & Indigenous American	0.0%	⌄
0.2%	● Unassigned	0.1%	

23andMe Ancestry Composition Chromosome Painting

The best feature offered by 23andMe in conjunction with ethnicity is providing testers with Ancestry Composition Chromosome Painting.[92]

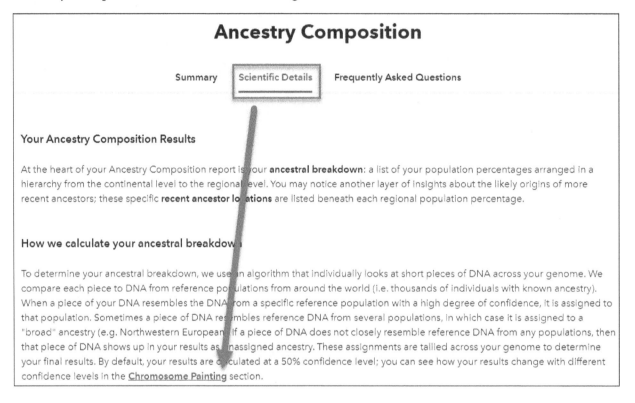

Your Ancestry Composition Chromosome Painting report is accessible under either Scientific Details or Ancestry Overview.

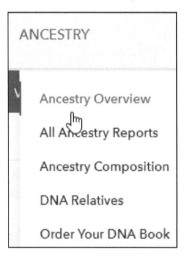

---

[92] https://dna-explained.com/2019/08/29/native-american-minority-ancestors-identified-using-dnapainter-plus-ethnicity-segments/

You'll want to select DNA Painting.

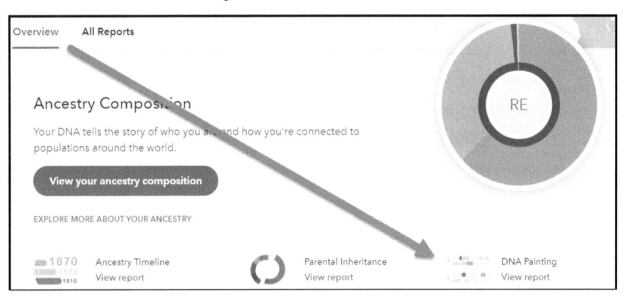

Testers can adjust their ethnicity confidence level within the Chromosome Painting function, just above chromosome 1.

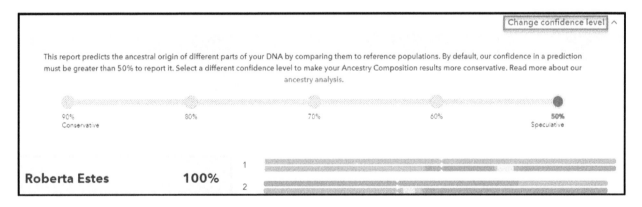

Adjusting the confidence level to 90% from 50% made no difference in my Native DNA reported, either in the amount or the location. This means that even though it's a small amount of Native DNA, 23andMe is highly confident that it is accurate.

Roberta Estes	100%
European	**99.5%**
Northwestern European	98.3%
French & German	63.3%
British & Irish	31.6%
Broadly Northwestern European	3.4%
Southern European	1.2%
Italian	1.2%
Trace Ancestry	**0.3%**

We detected traces of the following populations in your DNA. Read more about trace ancestry in the FAQ.

Native American	0.3%
Unassigned	**0.2%**
No Data Available	

On the left side of your Chromosome Painting results is a color-coded legend for the painting, which is shown on the right side of the page.

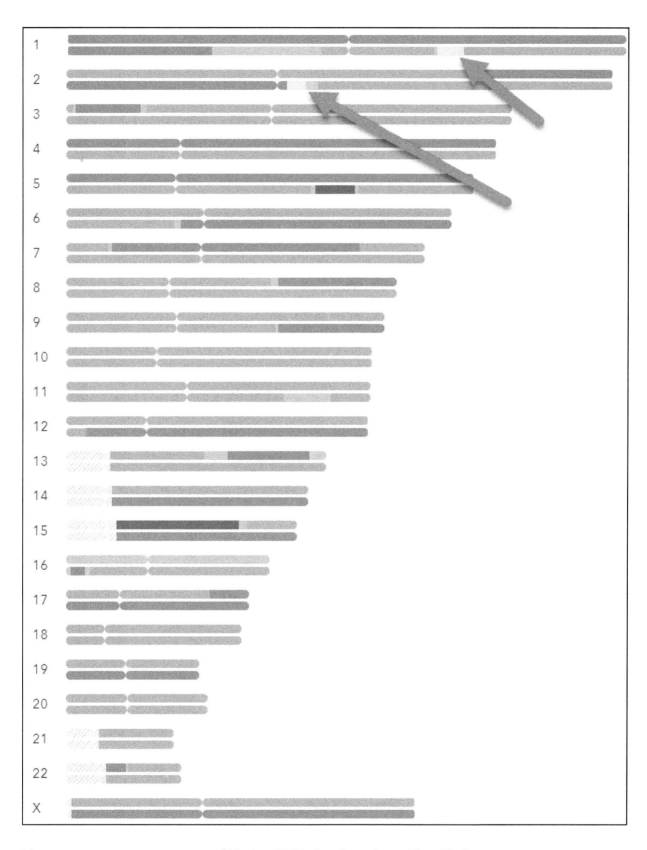

I have two separate segments of Native DNA that have been identified.

Remember that every person has two chromosomes, one from each parent. 23andMe attempts to position the segments on the proper "side," using academic phasing, but unless at least one of your parents actually tests, 23andMe simply has to make its best effort. If your parents test, 23andMe can generally position your segments properly, although not always.

If you have more than one Native segment, it's possible that you inherited segments from both parents. It's also possible that the segments are incorrectly positioned. In the version shown above, both of my segments are shown on the lower chromosome, but in another "updated" version, one segment is shown on the upper chromosome and one on the lower.

Remember that each chromosome is phased independently. Don't interpret finding a specific ethnicity on the upper side of one chromosome and the bottom of another chromosome to mean both parents carry that ethnicity.

Testers cannot assume that the top chromosome is always one specific parent's and the bottom is the other. In the case shown below, my mother's Native segment is displayed on the top segment of chromosome 1 and on the bottom segment of chromosome 2.

Without at least one parent testing, 23andMe has no way to know whether your top chromosome of any pair is mother or father, and it may reassemble the various segments incorrectly. The position, top or bottom, may also change from version to version.

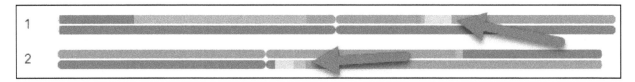

23andMe does paint the X chromosome, which has a very specific inheritance path.[93] Women inherit an X chromosome from both parents, but males inherit an X chromosome only from their mother.[94] If you carry Native American DNA on your X chromosome, the inheritance path will assist you greatly in eliminating several ancestors on both sides of your tree as donors, but only for X segments.

Don't confuse the X chromosome with mitochondrial DNA, both of which have a specific, unique, and different inheritance path.[95]

DNAPainter and Ethnicity

Both 23andMe and FamilyTreeDNA provide customers with the ability to download their ethnicity segments.

DNAPainter, a popular web-based application, provides the ability to map your DNA that has been identified as having descended from specific ancestors. Additionally, you can upload your ethnicity

---

[93] https://dna-explained.com/2017/02/07/using-x-and-mitochondrial-dna-charts-by-charting-companion/
[94] https://dna-explained.com/2012/09/27/x-marks-the-spot/
[95] https://dna-explained.com/2017/07/26/x-matching-and-mitochondrial-dna-is-not-the-same-thing/

segments in one bulk file. Adding your ethnicity segments to your painted segments facilitates identifying the ancestors from whom your Native DNA descends.

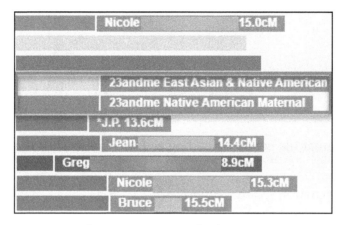

I painted my Native segment on chromosome 1, which originates on my mother's side. I then painted the matches that could be identified as maternal and assigned earliest known ancestors via color coding. This technique allowed me to associate my Native segments with the Acadian couple Honore Lord/Lore and his wife, Marie LaFaille. The French Acadians settled on Nova Scotia in about 1604 and were known to intermarry with the Mi'kmaq people until 1755, when the Acadians were forcibly removed by the English.

Following the ancestors of Honore Lord and Marie LaFaille back in time, I was able to confirm at least one Native ancestor eight generations ago using Y and mitochondrial DNA, along with original records.

To paint your 23andMe ethnicity segments at DNAPainter, you'll need to download the 23andMe file that holds your Ancestry Composition segment data.

At 23andMe, beneath your painted DNA segments, in the section "Do more with your Ancestry Composition results," you'll see View Scientific Details.

At the bottom of the next page, you'll see the link to download your raw Ancestry Composition data.

Download your Ancestry Composition raw data for even more information. Genomic coordinates (NCBI Build 37) for your Ancestry Composition results are available in CSV format.

Select Confidence Level ⓘ   50% ⌄

Download Raw Data

You don't need to open that file before uploading to DNAPainter, but the contents of the file will show the following:

- The assigned population (Native American)
- Which side or copy of each chromosome 23andMe has assigned that particular segment (Copy 2)
- Which chromosome(s) (chr1, chr2)
- The start and end points of that particular population segment

Ancestry	Copy	Chromosome	Start Point	End Point
Native American	2	chr1	164354594	176362201
Native American	2	chr2	97877591	106243696

I've written several articles about using DNAPainter, which can be found in a summary article titled, "DNAPainter Instructions and Resources,"[96] and I've specifically addressed identifying Native American ancestors in the article titled, "Native American and Minority Ancestors Identified Using DNAPainter Plus Ethnicity Segments."[97]

DNAPainter does ask you if you know which "side" is maternal and paternal. Be careful, remembering that the top and bottom of every chromosome may not be uniformly maternal or paternal.

DNAPainter is currently implementing an import for FamilyTreeDNA's painted ethnicity segments so that they can be painted at once in a bulk import using the segment download file described in the FamilyTreeDNA section.

If you haven't started using DNAPainter, this would be a wonderful time.[98]

---

[96] https://dna-explained.com/2019/10/14/dnapainter-instructions-and-resources/
[97] https://dna-explained.com/2019/08/29/native-american-minority-ancestors-identified-using-dnapainter-plus-ethnicity-segments/
[98] https://dnapainter.com/blog/why-map-your-chromosomes/

Autosomal DNA Matching

DNA matching is the lynchpin of autosomal testing; however, using matching to identify an unknown Native American ancestor may be difficult.

Generally, if someone's Native ancestor is close in time, meaning the closest few generations, they already know the identity of that person and that they were Native. If your grandparent is Native, you likely know where they lived, what tribe they were a member of, and so forth.

In the United States, the census identified people who were "Indian" and did not live on reservations. A category specified as "Indians not-taxed" began in 1860. These individuals would generally have been mixed race people who were still socially identified as Indians in their community and remained tribally affiliated.[99]

People living in 1860 would be four or five generations ago. Their living descendants today would be between fourth and sixth cousins, sharing 1% or less of their DNA.[100] Some cousins at that relationship level will share some DNA above a match threshold,[101] but others will share none. Furthermore, if your ancestor was already admixed, you might share some of their DNA, but perhaps not from their Native ancestors.

In other words, if that ancestor in 1860 was already admixed, then the amount of Native DNA that their descendants carry would be less, as would your chances of inheriting Native DNA.

Indians "not taxed" generally meant those living on reservations. Native people living on reservations were enumerated in a special Indian census beginning in 1885.[102] Unfortunately, the Indian census records were not reliably taken, and some tribes were excluded.[103] The good news is that later years also provided the "degree of blood," meaning the amount Native that they were "by blood"—for example, ¾ or 15/16. People living on reservations were more likely to be fully Native, but many were already admixed as well.

If you're among the genealogists who don't know the identity of their Native ancestor, general DNA matching will likely be the last tool you'll use. The best use for autosomal DNA matching to identify Native ancestors is after you've identified Native DNA segments.

Then, at vendors who support segment information (meaning not at Ancestry[104]), you can do the following:

- Identify which of your matches are from that parent's side.

---

[99] https://eric.ed.gov/?id=EJ751642

[100] https://dnapainter.com/tools/sharedcmv4

[101] Minimum match thresholds vary at vendors from 6-8 cM of contiguous DNA and may change from time to time.

[102] https://www.archives.gov/research/census/native-americans

[103] https://www.familysearch.org/wiki/en/American_Indian_Census_Rolls

[104] Ancestry does not provide segment information, such as segment start and end addresses, which precludes determining other people who match you on your Native segments.

- Determine which people match you on that Native segment. They will also show that segment as Native American.

- See which people you match in common with those people.

- Triangulate on that segment, confirming a common ancestor between multiple people.

- Identify common ancestors between you and the other people you match/triangulate with on that segment.

- Search for common locations for multiple people who share that Native segment.

- Reach out to your matches on that segment with the hope they will know the identity of their Native ancestor, supported by evidence. Their Native ancestor may be your Native ancestor or family too.

Additionally, you can identify cousins who carry the Y or mitochondrial DNA of your ancestor, which will allow you to confirm that your common ancestor was, or was not, Native.

DNA Matching and Endogamy

Both endogamy and pedigree collapse[105] can affect autosomal matching, especially in individuals who are fully Native, meaning not admixed.

Endogamy occurs when a population as a whole has been isolated and community members intermarried extensively and exclusively within the population. This leads to population members inheriting many of the same segments of DNA because their historical ancestors prior to a genealogical time frame are the same. This is especially evident when viewing smaller segments, below the vendor matching thresholds, but is often evident in other ways as well.

In groups where many people have tested, people from endogamous populations will have many more matches than people from non-endogamous populations. We see examples of this routinely in people with Jewish and Acadian ancestry, who often have twice as many matches as people with ancestry from non-endogamous populations.

However, the converse can be true too. Often, Native American people, especially those with little or no admixture, have fewer matches because a low proportion of Native American people have taken DNA tests.

Pedigree collapse is the same concept, except in a more recent time frame. Pedigree collapse refers to sharing known ancestors on different branches of your family. When pedigree collapse occurs, you're more likely to retain segments from that ancestral couple because they contributed their DNA through multiple ancestral lines. In small communities where people seldom move away or marry outside the community, pedigree collapse and endogamy are both common.

---

[105] https://dna-explained.com/2021/07/23/whats-the-difference-between-pedigree-collapse-and-endogamy/

In practical terms, this means fully Native people are likely to match several people on both maternal and paternal lines, especially in smaller tribes, either due to endogamy or pedigree collapse.

Partially Native people may have a high number of matches to a highly tested Native endogamous group, such as Acadians. You may have few matches to a poorly tested tribe or community, or one with very few remaining members. In some cases, you may match people with Native ancestry but not be able to find a common ancestor, because your common ancestor occurred before genealogical records.

PART 4

MITOCHONDRIAL DNA –
ANCIENT *and* MODERN

Now, let's discuss the different kinds of DNA tests you can utilize for discovering or confirming Native American heritage.

Indigenous American Mitochondrial DNA

Mitochondrial DNA is inherited by both males and females from their mother.

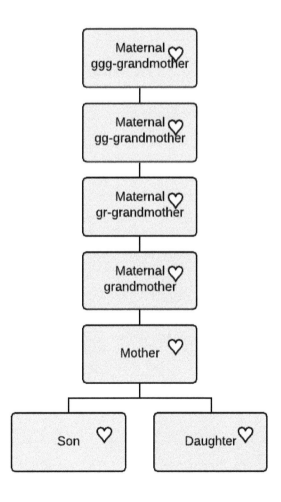

Only women pass mitochondrial DNA, shown in the chart on the previous page, by the little heart, to their descendants, so everyone's mitochondrial DNA descends from their direct matrilineal line—your mother, her mother, her mother, on up your tree.

Mitochondrial DNA never recombines with the father's DNA.

If your direct matrilineal ancestor was Native American on her mother's side, then her haplogroup (her genetically related group) will be one of the known and proven indigenous Native haplogroups. Proven Native American haplogroups include portions of haplogroups A, B, C, D, and X.

Some haplogroup subgroups, or subclades of the aforementioned haplogroups, are proven to be Native and some are not, resulting in confusion. In other words, everyone in haplogroup A is not Native American, but within haplogroup A, subgroup A2 and downstream haplogroups—such as A2a, A2b, and so forth—are proven to be Native. In addition to current testers, legitimate Native American haplogroups have been identified in ancient remains as well.

No haplogroups other than subgroups of A, B, C, D, and X have been found in ancient remains in the Americas. Put another way, if other haplogroups were found among the Native people before contact with Europeans, then we would find ancient DNA in Native burials that includes haplogroups other than the ones I've mentioned, unless those other haplogroups were extremely rare.

If someone tells you that they have a different Native American haplogroup, take that with an entire salt lick. There is no evidence whatsoever of known European haplogroups among Native people before contact.

Let me provide a very clear example—there is absolutely no evidence that the most common European male haplogroup, R, and the most common European mitochondrial haplogroup, H, are Native American. Conversely, there is overwhelming evidence through scientific research and DNA matches that these haplogroups are found today in Europe, not in the Native population. If your ancestor is Native American and has been separated from people on the Eurasian continent for ten thousand years, give or take a thousand or two, you won't have exact or even close matches with people living there today.[106] After European contact, some adoptions into tribes did occur, but for the most part, when people with Native American ancestry test and find European haplogroups, it results from mistaken attribution.

I provide a comprehensive resource on the DNAeXplain website in the article, "Native American Mitochondrial Haplogroups."[107] Just type the article name in the search box or use the URL in the footnote below.

Let's discuss how haplogroups are formed.

---

[106] https://dna-explained.com/2016/09/14/haplogroup-x2b4-is-european-not-native-american/
[107] https://dna-explained.com/2013/09/18/native-american-mitochondrial-haplogroups/

Mitochondrial Haplogroup Formation

For genealogists, it's easiest to think about haplogroup formation in similar terms to our family pedigree charts.

Parents have children, who then have children, forming generations and ancestral pedigree charts reaching back as far as we can identify ancestors. Haplogroups are formed the same way, with new SNP (Single Nucleotide Polymorphism) mutations in the parent's generation providing the new offspring haplogroups. Every generation, beginning with that offspring haplogroup, will carry the mutation that the offspring had. Mutations accumulate over time.

FamilyTreeDNA provides a free public Mitochondrial DNA tree[108] that includes each haplogroup and the self-identified countries of origin flags for testers' ancestors.

For example, here's haplogroup A through A2.[109]

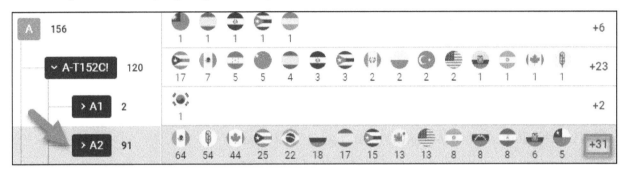

The number of subgroups, subclades, or child haplogroups is noted beside the haplogroup name. Haplogroup A has a total of 156 downstream haplogroups, not all shown here.

Haplogroup A-T152C! has 120 child haplogroups. Their "child," A1, has two additional child haplogroups.

Haplogroup A2 is where Native American haplogroups are found in haplogroup A. A2 contains 91 child haplogroups. Click on any haplogroup to expand.

Flags where testers' earliest known ancestors are found are shown to the right of the haplogroup. Mouse over any flag to view the country. Not all flags can always be displayed.

You'll notice that for haplogroup A2, above, there are an additional 31 locations at far right, or flags not shown. You can access those by clicking on the +31 or the detailed Country Report, shown on the next page, available to the right of the 31 by clicking on the three dots.

---

[108] https://www.familytreedna.com/public/mt-dna-haplotree/L
[109] https://www.familytreedna.com/public/mt-dna-haplotree/A;name=A2

Country Report: mtDNA Haplogroup A2				
Maternal Origin*	Branch Participants A2	Downstream Participants A2 and Downstream (Excluding other Letters)	All Downstream Participants A2 and Downstream (Including other Letters)	Distribution
(+) Mexico	64	406	406	29.90%
United States (Native American)	54	238	238	17.53%
Puerto Rico	25	147	147	10.82%

The first three entries of the haplogroup A2 Country Report show that almost 30% of the ancestors of people with haplogroup A2 (and no further subgroup) are found in Mexico in the FamilyTreeDNA database.

Remember that ancestral locations are "self-identified" by the tester under Account Settings/Genealogy/Earliest Known Ancestors. Both the United States and Canada have designations for the country generally, and specifically for Native ancestors with that country. The concept is that if your earliest ancestor is found in the United States, you'll just select "United States," but if they are indigenous to the United States, you'll select a Native option.

The following selections are provided for the United States and Canada:

- United States
- United States (Kānaka Maoli), meaning Native Hawaiian
- United States (Native American), identified by a feather
- Canada
- Canada (First Nations), identified by a maple leaf flag with a feather
- Canada (Inuit)

The Native designation is a valuable resource, but like any genealogical reporting, it's subject to both misunderstanding and error.

Some people don't understand that a matrilineal ancestor is not the same as a "maternal" ancestor and provide information for the wrong person. Maternal could be anyone on your mother's side of the tree, while matrilineal means through the direct mother-to-mother line.

Some people simply have incorrect information in their tree. Some people provide what they believe to be true, but isn't. For example, many people in Mexico report their ancestors to be Spanish or from the Canary Islands, but after DNA testing, some of those "Spanish" ancestors turn out to be aboriginal Native. Often people don't think about updating their information and selecting another designation, not realizing that incorrect information is being displayed to other people.

This is also the source of some of the myths about European haplogroups being Native American. For example, you'll find a single United States Native "feather" on many proven European haplogroups because testers believe, before testing, that their great-great-grandmother was Native

American. I wrote about the process of determining whether a haplogroup is European or Native American in the article titled, "Haplogroup X2b4 is European, Not Native American."[110]

Let's look at haplogroup A2 as an example. I searched for the A2 branch on the public mitochondrial tree[111] to illustrate the descendancy of haplogroup A subgroups.

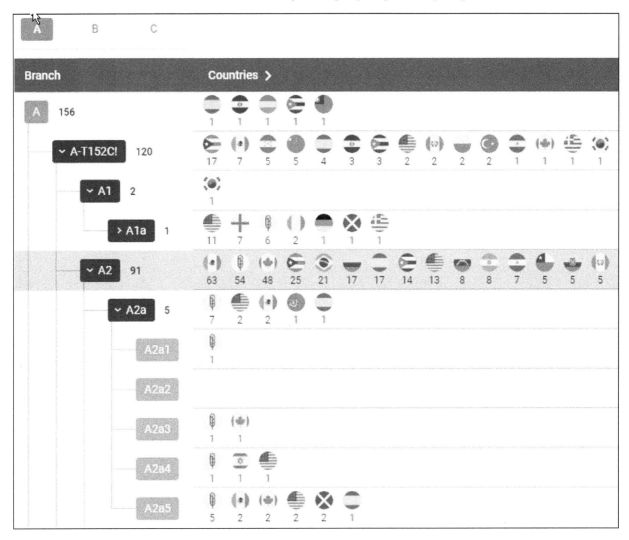

A woman who lived approximately 150,000 years ago[112] in Africa is the common matrilineal ancestor of all living people today.[113] Known as Mitochondrial Eve, she wasn't the first women to live, but she is the first women to have children who survived to populate the world. She had ancestors, of course, and probably siblings and aunts and uncles like the rest of us—but only

---

[110] https://dna-explained.com/2016/09/14/haplogroup-x2b4-is-european-not-native-american/
[111] https://www.familytreedna.com/public/mt-dna-haplotree/A;name=A2
[112] Date refined by the Million Mito Project team
[113] https://www.nature.com/articles/nature.2013.13478

her children survived to the present day. She is the MRCA (most recent common ancestor) of everyone.

How do we know this? Because we can track mutations back in time to her. Just like we are the "leaves" of our ancestors on our family tree, members of haplogroups today are the leaves on the branches of Mitochondrial Eve, both literally and in a mitochondrial genetic sense.

Of course, we'll never be able to extend our actual genealogy back that far in time, but our genetic tree does reach back that distantly, and we can track it through the breadcrumb trail of cumulative mutations.

FamilyTreeDNA also provides a list of defining mutations for each haplogroup.[114]

Haplogroups				Defining Mutations
A				A235G, A663G, A1736G, T4248C, A4824G, C8794T, C16290T, G16319A
	A-T152C!			T152C!
		A2		T146C!, C152T!!, A153G, G8027A, G12007A, C16111T
			A2a	C3330T, C16192T
			A2a1	C16261T
			A2a2	C9301T
			A2a3	T16311C!
			A2a4	G5460A, T16093C
			A2a5	T3552C, T12166C, A16233G, A16331G, C16362T!

This table shows the defining V17 haplogroup mutation locations in the mitochondria for each of the haplogroup branches shown above. The mitochondrial haplotree has version numbers, with V17 being the version in use in 2021. New scientific discoveries are incorporated into each new tree version, sometimes resulting in branch renaming. The Million Mito Project, now underway, will provide an updated tree.

Every haplogroup is defined by all the mutations in the preceding haplogroups on the tree, plus the mutations that are unique to its own branch. Haplogroup A2, for example, includes all the mutations of haplogroup A, the mutations of the haplogroup upstream (A-T152C!), and the defining mutations of haplogroup A2 itself. Anyone with all those cumulative mutations will be assigned to haplogroup A2. If a tester has additional mutations that have been assigned to a haplogroup, such as the two mutations in haplogroup A2a, then that's their home haplogroup. If you also have mutation C16261T, then A2a1 is your haplogroup.

FamilyTreeDNA is the only company to test your full mitochondrial DNA, which is necessary to assign a complete haplogroup and required for comprehensive comparison to other testers.

---

[114] https://www.familytreedna.com/mtDNA-Haplogroup-Mutations.aspx

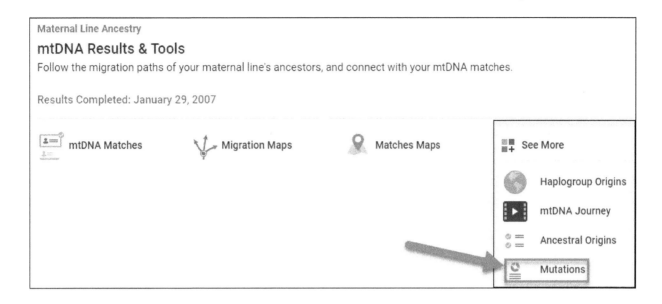

Generally, people have "extra" mutations, viewable under the See More tab, then the Mutations link. Extra mutations are not (currently) used to define haplogroups, but as multiple people test who have extra mutations, these extra mutations will be the seeds of future haplogroups.

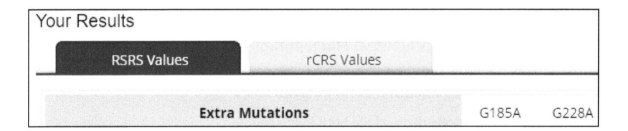

You may find some of those extra mutations grouped together to identify a new haplogroup in future releases. If you're interested in the mitochondrial PhyloTree itself, along with the history of the tree structure, you can read all about that at phylotree.org.[115]

Some haplogroups have not been named in the standard A, A2, A2a branching tree structure. Haplogroup A-T152C! is a perfect example. It was discovered after the structure of A, and then A2, was defined. Haplogroup A-T152C! could not be inserted in the tree between A and A2 without renaming the substructure beneath haplogroup A, including A2 and everything beneath. Therefore, haplogroup A-T152C! was inserted in the tree using the name of its only defining mutation instead of disrupting the tree structure, which would have meant renaming every A2 and downstream haplogroup assigned to people who had already tested.

To be clear, renaming sometimes does occur when new tree versions are released, but scientists try to avoid disruption whenever possible. Not only does wholesale renaming confuse consumers, it also makes earlier academic publications difficult, if not impossible, to follow. When possible,

---

[115] http://phylotree.org/

scientists simply add to existing haplogroups by adding another letter or number. For example, haplogroup Z2b might become Z2b1.[116]

Having said that, check your haplogroup periodically, and always after a new mitochondrial tree version is released, to see if your haplogroup has been updated. If so, that means progress has been made refining the tree, and there may be good surprises waiting for you in your match list. At the full sequence level at FamilyTreeDNA, you'll only match people with your own extended haplogroup and with a limited number of mutations, called "genetic distance."

The more the branching tree structure can be refined, the more we can tell testers about their matrilineal ancestors and where they lived during periods in the past. That veil of time before existing records cannot be pierced any other way. Conversely, more recently occurring mutations can be utilized to focus on specific geographies and, sometimes, to the family level.

The next revision of the mitochondrial tree will be published through the Million Mito Project, a collaborative team effort between Dr. Paul Maier, Population Geneticist, and Goran Runfeldt, Head of R&D, both at FamilyTreeDNA; Dr. Miguel Vilar, former Lead Scientist for the National Geographic Genographic Project; and me.[117] The new Million Mito Tree of Womankind will be based on hundreds of thousands of samples, not just a few thousand—hence the name, the "Million Mito Project." We're hoping to reach a million full sequence testers before the publication of the new tree. You can participate by taking a full sequence mitochondrial DNA test at FamilyTreeDNA.

Indigenous American Mitochondrial Haplogroups

I provide a page on DNAexplain that lists and maintains indigenous American haplogroups discovered and documented through the following resources:

- Academic publications that include both living people/populations and ancient DNA

- Thousands of National Geographic Genographic Project testers who opted in to research

- Native American, haplogroup specific, and geographic projects at FamilyTreeDNA that include indigenous DNA results and whose members have allowed their results to be included in public project pages

- Ancient and contemporary DNA samples from academic publications uploaded to GenBank,[118] referenced in PhyloTree Build 17 and earlier[119]

I've mapped the various Native haplogroups. Let's start with ancient DNA for each haplogroup because the location of ancient remains provides us with a base map of migration. We know when those people lived in that location.

---

[116] There is no mitochondrial haplogroup Z, which is why I selected this as an example to avoid confusion.
[117] https://dna-explained.com/2020/03/17/the-million-mito-project/
[118] https://www.ncbi.nlm.nih.gov/genbank/
[119] http://www.phylotree.org/

Some of the ancient DNA sample information was compiled by Jean Manco before her death, followed by Carlos Quiles.[120] Additional ancient sample information has been extracted from academic papers not included in those summaries.

Each of the Native haplogroups—mitochondrial haplogroups A, B, C, D, and X, along with Y DNA haplogroups Q and C—have somewhat different migration routes. The information we can extrapolate from these ancient samples is both fascinating and informative.

For many years, researchers debated whether the first people to inhabit North and South America arrived in one migration or in multiple waves.

Consensus today—based in part on the haplogroup distribution, ancient DNA ages, and the fact that the Inuit followed a circumpolar route and are not found elsewhere in North, Central, or South America—is that there were multiple waves. If all the indigenous ancestors arrived together, their migration routes throughout the Americas would have been similar.

For each haplogroup, I've mapped both ancient DNA as well as contemporary DNA from various sources, including academic papers, the Genographic Project, publicly available sources, and FamilyTreeDNA projects where members have opted in to allow their ancestors' locations to be displayed publicly.

On the maps, each location was mapped one time, regardless of how many samples or how many haplogroup subclades of that haplogroup are found in that location. Therefore, one pin might represent several samples obtained from multiple studies or testers. For example, many people selected "Mexico" if they weren't certain of a more specific location. Mexico will be mapped one time, but literally thousands of people could have listed Mexico as the location.

When viewing ancient DNA maps of the United States, keep in mind that archaeological excavations are complex and have a painful history in the Native community. Remains were often taken to universities or museums, or they were destroyed by grave-robbers or otherwise desecrated without involving Native people. Contemporary tribes are often hesitant to authorize DNA testing of the remains of their ancestors.[121]

Tribal affiliations and locations are provided by academic researchers or the consumers who tested.

The following are resources used to compile the ancient and modern haplogroup charts:

- Samples uploaded to GenBank and references on phylotree.org

- Various public projects at FamilyTreeDNA

- Academic publications

---

[120] https://indo-european.eu/ancient-dna/
[121] https://www.nps.gov/subjects/nagpra/index.htm

- Public Genographic Project samples, as detailed in the "New Native Mitochondrial DNA Haplogroups"[122] article

- Genographic samples opted in for research at the close of the public participation portion of the Genographic Project

- The public mitochondrial DNA tree provided by FamilyTreeDNA[123]

Mitochondrial DNA Native Haplogroup A

Ancient Mitochondrial Haplogroup A

Ancient haplogroup A samples are found in Russia and Mongolia, near Lake Baikal, where the people who became the first Native aboriginal people of the Americas are believed to have originated. Some subgroups of haplogroup A spread westward from the Lake Baikal region into eastern Europe, specifically to what is now Hungary, but they are rare and easy to differentiate from haplogroups that spread east from the Lake Baikal region into Siberia and, eventually, crossed Beringia into North America.

---

[122] https://dna-explained.com/2017/03/02/new-native-american-mitochondrial-dna-haplogroups/
[123] https://www.familytreedna.com/public/mt-dna-haplotree/A

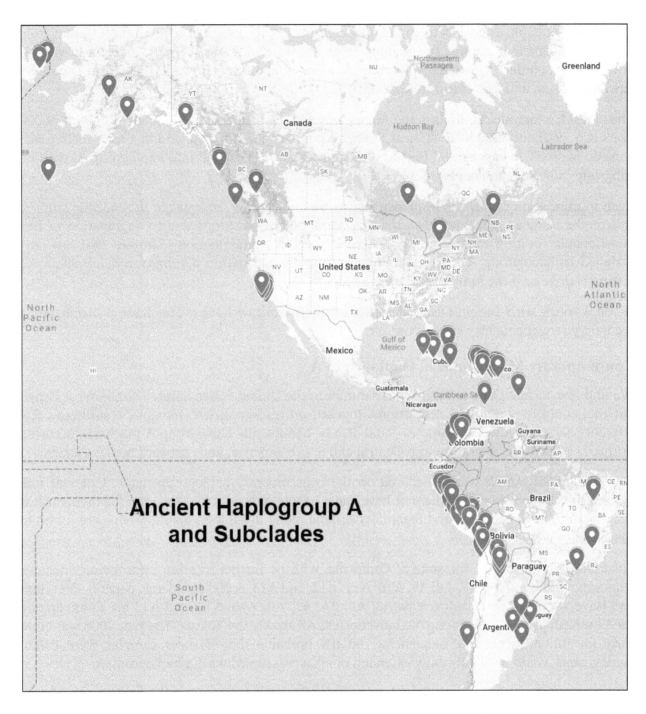

Ancient Haplogroup A and Subclades

At least one migration path for ancient haplogroup A in the Americas along the Pacific coastline becomes obvious when viewing the cluster on the western coast of South America. Peru has been the focus of several academic studies, so testing bias may play a part in the number of samples found in that region. The Caribbean Islands were settled by Native people from northern South America and into Brazil.[124]

<hr>

[124] https://en.wikipedia.org/wiki/Indigenous_peoples_of_the_Caribbean

While ancient haplogroup A is the most prevalent in South America, it's not entirely absent from North America and likely was swept along by an eastward migration across Canada near what is now the US border. We find haplogroup A along the water pathway—the Great Lakes, St. Lawrence River, and into Maritime Canada.

The oldest haplogroup A burials in the Americas are in the Lauricocha Highlands[125] of Peru (9,000 years ago, or about 7000 BCE[126]), near the headwaters of the Amazon, and in a rock shelter site, Lapa do Santo,[127] in east-central Brazil (10,000 years ago). These fall into haplogroup A, with no subgroup indicated, and haplogroup A2.

Keep in mind though that full sequence testing was not always undertaken in academic studies, and/or the samples may have been missing some marker locations due to degradation or had questionable location calls removed due to suspected contamination. Samples that are only assigned to haplogroup A, without a subgroup, might fall within a subgroup if full sequence testing is done or if the sample is not degraded.

When working with ancient DNA, scientists can only work with what they have available, and a secondary sequencing may not be possible.

Contemporary Mitochondrial Haplogroup A

We find few ancient DNA haplogroup A samples in the United States, limited to the West Coast, but that could be due to the restrictions imposed on testing ancient remains, resulting in few reference samples. A lack of samples could also be because the haplogroup A migration occurred primarily as a coastal migration into Central and South America, and eastward across Canada.

Each individual sample was not placed on the contemporary haplogroup maps. One star was placed for each location, regardless of how many people indicated that location for their earliest known matrilineal ancestor, and regardless of how many A haplogroup subgroups are found in that location.

For example, the star for the state of California, with no further location information, includes haplogroups A3, A5, A6, A7, A8, A9, A10, A11, A12, and A13. A 2009 academic paper by Breschini and Haversat noted that haplogroups A3, A5, A6, A7, A9, A10, A12, and A13 are found among the Chumash people, A11 among the Luiseno, and A8 among the Yokuts. The year 2008 was quite early for full mitochondrial sequencing, so it's probable that if these samples were rerun, haplogroups would be significantly extended or even reassigned within haplogroup A.

It's interesting to note that both Greenland samples fall into haplogroup A2b1, which is also found in these locations:

- Ekven, Russia, burials on the Chukotka Peninsula, the easternmost Russian peninsula, closest to Alaska

---

[125] https://en.wikipedia.org/wiki/Lauricocha_culture
[126] BCE means before the current era which began at the year 0, so the functional equivalent of BC.
[127] https://en.wikipedia.org/wiki/Lapa_do_Santo

- Alaska, noted as Inuit

- Noted as found in the "United States," but with no additional information

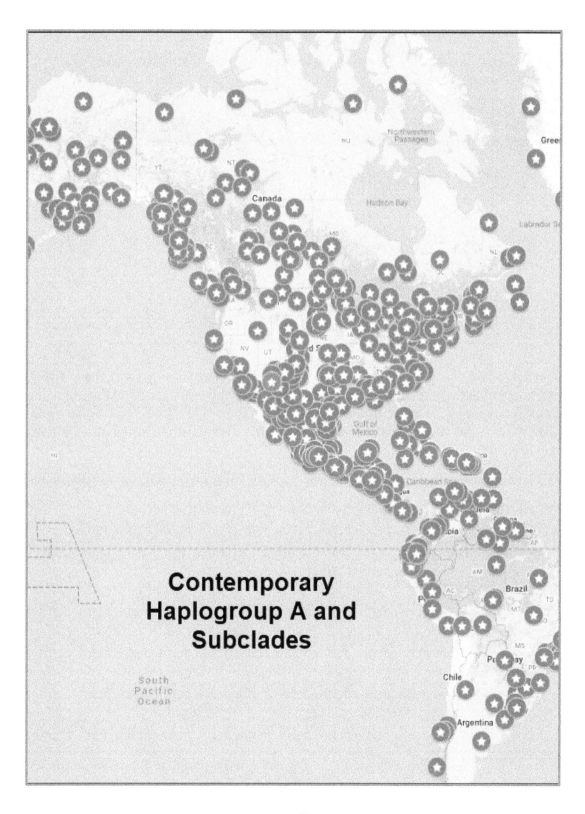

Contemporary
Haplogroup A and
Subclades

It's important to understand the value of full sequence testing. Every single sample from the Americas that has been fully sequenced beyond haplogroup A is either A2 or a subclade of A2.

Given that, it's tempting for researchers to assume that any haplogroup they notice that is A2, or any A2 subclade, is Native American, but that's incorrect.

For example, we find two A2a3 samples dating from about 1200 CE in Mongolia.

However, we also find two A2a3 samples in the Highlands of Peru dating from about 4,200 years ago. It's quite possible that the further evaluation occurring in the Million Mito Project will assign these samples more specific haplogroups that will separate them from each other. For now, genealogists need to be very careful not to assume that every sample assigned to a particular haplogroup is Native.

- All Native Americans with mitochondrial haplogroup A fall into A2 or subclades, but…

- Not all haplogroup A2 subclades are exclusively indigenous American.

The public mitochondrial tree at FamilyTreeDNA[128] is a good resource to see where haplogroups of current testers—and ancient or academic samples of sufficient quality to be included—are found in the world.

---

[128] https://www.familytreedna.com/public/mt-dna-haplotree/L

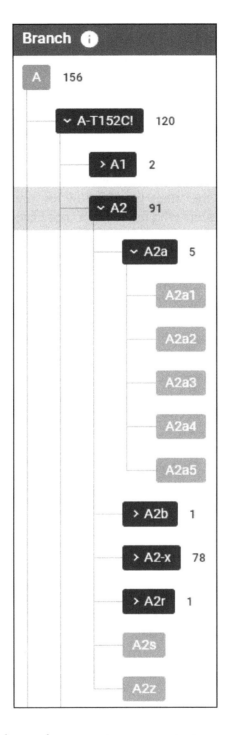

Today, the public mitochondrial tree shows contemporary testers with haplogroup A2a3 as Native in the United States (which includes Alaska) and Canada.[129] No ancient or academic samples have yet been included for haplogroup A2a3, but there are plans to add them to the tree in a future update.

---

[129] https://www.familytreedna.com/public/mt-dna-haplotree/A;name=A2a3

Haplogroup A Tribal Affiliations

In the following chart, Identified Haplogroups are displayed along with the ancestral or current tribe listed by testers, scientists, or academic researchers.

As expected, many samples are assigned to haplogroup A, with no further subgroup identified. That suggests that a subgroup would be assigned if further testing is undertaken. Regardless, we know they are found in haplogroup A.

Some rows have multiple haplogroups listed, which means that those tribes were represented in those multiple haplogroups. All the tribes listed below for any Identified Haplogroups category have either academic papers or testers who fall in all of those haplogroups and have indicated their descent from one of those tribes:

Tribe	Identified Haplogroups
Aleut (Alaska), Alutiiq (Alaska), Apache, Arawak (Guyana, Aruba), Assiniboine (Montana), Athabascan, Aztec (Mexico), Blackfoot (Alberta), Carib (Trinidad and Tobago), Cherokee, Cheyenne, Chibcha (Colombia), Chippewa (Canada, US), Choctaw, Choco (Panama), Chowanoc/PeeDee, Coastal Salish, Coca (Mexico), Cree (Canada), Dakota Sioux, Dene-tha (Northwest Territories), Eyak Gwich'in (Northwest Territories), Haida, Huetar, Inuit (Labrador, Nunavut and Greenland), Inupiaq, Inuvialuit (Canadian Arctic), Kaska, Kwakiutl (Canada), Lakota, Lenca (El Salvador), Marajoara (Brazil), Mayan, Mazahua, Menominee, Mi'kmaq, Mixe (Oaxaca), Mohawk, Navajo, Nuu-Chah-Nulth First Nations (British Columbia), Oglala Lakota, Ojibwa (Canada, US), Onondaga, Potawatomi, Seminole, Seneca, Tahltan (British Columbia), Taino (Puerto Rico), Tarahumara, Tarascan (Mexico), Tlingit, Tsimshian (Canada), Winnebago, Yaqui, Yupik (Siberia, Alaska), Zapotec, Zenu (Colombia)	A
Ache, Arsario, Athabascan, Canada, Carib (Dominica), Cayapa, Chickasaw, Dogrib, Guarani, Haida, Interior Salish (British Columbia), Inupiaq, Katuena, Kayapo, Kwakuitl First Nations, Lenape, Mayan (El Salvador, Guatemala), Narragansett, Poturu, Seminole, Shuswop, Slave Lake Cree, Surui, Taku River Tlingit (British Columbia), Tlicho, Tlingit, Waiwai, Yupik, Zapotec, Zoro	A2

Cherokee, Choctaw, Cree, Cree/Chippewa Huron, Mi'kmaq, Ottawa/Odawa, PeeDee	A, A2f1a
Chitimacha	A, A2-T16189C!, A2ad
Choctaw	A, A2, A2-C64T
Algonquian	A2, A2n
Taino	A2, A2ah, A2am, A2d1, A2k1a, A2z
Selkup (Russia)	A2a1
Chukchu (Chukotka Peninsula, Russia)	A2a1, A2a2
Inuit	A2, A2a, A2a1, A2a2, A2a3, A2b1,
Apache	A2, A2a, A2a4, A2a5, A2e, A2h1, A2q1
Copper Inuit (Nunavut, Canada), Inpuiaq	A2b1
Sioux	A2f1, A2n
Cree	A2f1a, A2a5, A2i
Chippewa, Mi'kmaq, Ojibwa	A2f1a
Tlinget	A2, A2-G16129A!
Inupiat (Alaska)	A2, A2b
Chumash	A2, A3, A5, A6, A7, A9, A10, A12
Aleut, Athabascan (Alaska), Na-Dene, Yupik	A2a
Cree, Na–Dene People (Northwest Territories), Shuswap	A2a5
Navajo	A2, A2a, A2a4, A2a5
Plains	A2a4
Aleut	A2a4
Apache First Nations, Athabascan, Secwepemc People (British Columbia)	A2a5
Quechuas (Peru)	A2aa
Cherokee	A2ab
Chukchi (Russia)	A2b
Chukchi (Russia), Inuit, Inuvialuit, Koryak	A2b1
Woodlands Cree (Alberta)	A2ao1
Chiricahua Apache, Eagle Wolf Tribe of Tlingit in Alaska	A2aq
Creek, Mayo Yoreme Tribe, Mexico	A2c
Cocama, Kogui, Yanomama	A2h
Chippewa, Kahnawake Mohawk (Quebec), Loon Lake Cree (Saskatchewan), Mi'kmaq, Ojibway, Sagkeeng First Nations (Manitoba), Sapotweyak Cree Nation (Manitoba)	A2i
Wauii	A2k
Pasto	A2k1a
Mayan (Belize)	A2m
Assiniboine, Batchewana First Nations, Blackfoot, Cheyenne, Cree, Cumberland House Saskatchewan Cree, Gros Ventre Ojibway	A2n

Lakota Sioux	A2q
California Native	A2q1
Tlicho	A2
Arsario, Guambiano, Kogi	A2w
Guaymi, La Tinta	A2w1
Creek	A2y
Yokuts	A8, A13
Luiseno	A11

Some haplogroup branches are named with the mutation that defines a subclade or branch. For example, A2-T16189C! means that the mutation T16189C! defines this subclade of A2. For an explanation of symbols such as exclamation marks and other mutation designations, please refer to the "Mitochondrial DNA Reference Page" on DNAeXplain[130] or the article "Mitochondrial DNA Part 2: What Do Those Numbers Mean?"[131]

As more people test, additional haplogroups will be found among various tribes.

Mitochondrial Haplogroup A - Ancient and Modern Samples Found in the Americas

Which haplogroups have been found in ancient DNA and modern testers in the Americas? I've compiled a chart showing both. Keep in mind that upper-level haplogroups like A and A2 may be a function of samples only being partially sequenced.

In South America, if more than four or five countries are represented, I simply list "South America," given that the haplogroup seems to be widely distributed across the continent. In the case of the United States, some studies and testers simply listed either "US" or "Canada," but in other cases, if the haplogroup distribution was widespread, I simply listed "US" instead of each state individually.

Haplogroup	Ancient & Region	Modern & Region
A	Yes – Americas	Yes – Americas
A-T152C!	No	Yes – Americas, some scattered Asia
A1	No	Questionable[132] – California, Korea, Mexico
A2	Yes – Americas	Yes – Americas
A2a	Yes – Alaska, Aleutian Islands, Caribbean, Chukotka in Russia, Puerto Rico, Western Canada	Yes – Alaska, Greenland, Labrador, Mexico, Oklahoma, Western US
A2a1	Yes – Chukotka in Russia, Alaska	Yes – Labrador, Newfoundland, US

[130] https://dna-explained.com/mitochondrial-dna/
[131] https://dna-explained.com/2019/05/23/mitochondrial-dna-part-2-what-do-those-numbers-mean/
[132] This haplogroup is generally found in Asia, so these people may have family who moved to the United States.

A2a2	Yes – Chukotka in Russia (Inuit)	Yes – Chukchu (Russia), Inuit
A2a3	Yes – Canada, Greenland, Mongolia, Peru	Yes – Northern North America, Russia
A2a4	No	Yes – Alaska, Aleutian Islands, Colombia, Mexico, Southwest US, US
A2a5	No	Yes – Alaska, Alberta, Arizona, Oklahoma, Canada, Ontario, Mexico, New Mexico, Northwest Territories, Texas, US
A2aa	No	Yes - Brazil, Panama, Peru
A2ab	No	Yes – Brazil, Georgia, North Carolina, Paraguay
A2ac	No	Yes – Colombia, Ecuador, Peru, Venezuela
A2ac1	No	Yes – Colombia, Cuba, Venezuela
A2ac2	No	Yes – Ecuador
A2ad	No	Yes – Cuba, Louisiana, Mexico, South America
A2ae	No	Yes – Guatemala, Mexico, Texas, US
A2af	No	Yes – Panama, Peru
A2af1	No	Yes – El Salvador
A2af1a	No	Yes – Canada, Colombia, Panama
A2af1a1	No	Yes – Colombia, Costa Rica, Mexico, Nicaragua, Panama, US
A2af1a2	No	Yes – Panama
A2af1b	No	Yes – Costa Rica, Mexico, Nicaragua, US
A2af1b1	No	Yes
A2af1b1b	No	Yes – Panama
A2af2	No	Yes – Nicaragua
A2ag	Yes – Alaska, British Columbia, Canada	Yes
A2ah	Yes – Argentina, British Columbia, Canada	Yes – Brazil, Peru, Puerto Rico
A2ai	No	Yes – Colombia, Mexico, US
A2aj	No	Yes – Mexico

A2ak	No	Yes – Canada, Colombia, Mexico, Ecuador, Peru, Puerto Rico, Venezuela, US
A2al	No	Yes –Argentina, Brazil, Colombia, Cuba, Mexico, Panama, Suriname
A2am	Yes - Curacao	Yes – Curacao, Dominican Republic, Peru, Puerto Rico, Trinidad and Tobago, Venezuela, US
A2an	No	Yes – Mexico
A2ao	Yes - Peru	Yes – Guatemala, Mexico, US
A2ao1	No	Yes – Alberta, Mexico, US
A2ap	No	Yes – Belize, El Salvador, Honduras, Guatemala, Mexico, Nicaragua, US
A2aq	Yes – British Columbia, Canada	Yes – Alaska, California, Ecuador, Mexico, US
A2ar	No	Yes – Ecuador, Guatemala, Peru
A2as	Yes – Peru	Yes – Peru
A2as1	No	Yes – Peru
A2at	No	Yes – Peru
A2at1	No	Yes – Peru
A2au	No	Yes – Peru
A2av	No	Yes – Mexico
A2av1	No	Yes – Ecuador, Peru
A2av1a	No	Yes – Ecuador, Peru, US
A2aw	No	Yes – Ecuador
A2b	No	Yes – Alaska
A2b1	No	Yes – Alaska, Canada, Greenland, Labrador, Northwest Territories, Newfoundland and Labrador, Nunuvut, US
A2c	No	Yes – Brazil, Cuba, Mexico, Peru, US
A2ca	Yes – California	No
A2cb	Yes – California	No
A2cc	Yes – California	No
A2-C64T	No	Yes – Canada, Cuba, Guatemala, Mexico, New Brunswick
A2d	Yes – British Columbia, Canada	Yes – Alaska, Canada, Cuba, Dominican Republic, El Salvador, Honduras, Mexico, Puerto Rico, Southwest US

A2d1	No	Yes - Cuba, El Salvador, Mexico, US
A2d1a	No	Yes – Honduras, Mexico, Michigan, New Mexico, Puerto Rico, US
A2d1a1	No	Yes
A2d2	No	Yes – Mexico, US
A2e	Yes – Brazil, Dominican Republic, Puerto Rico	Yes – Bolivia, Brazil, Ecuador, Mexico, Mississippi, New Mexico, US
A2f	No	Yes – Canada, Mexico, Puerto Rico, US
A2f1	No	Yes – Canada, Minnesota, Newfoundland, US
A2f1a	No	Yes – Alberta, Canada, Minnesota, Northern US, Ontario, Mexico, Nova Scotia
A2f2	No	Yes - Mexico
A2f3	No	Yes – Mexico, Puerto Rico, US
A2g	No	Yes – Cuba, Guatemala, Mexico, Southwest US
A2g1	No	Yes – Mexico, New Mexico, Texas, US
A2-G153A!	No	Yes – Brazil, Mexico, Quebec, Texas, US, Wisconsin
A2-G16129A!	No	Yes – Alaska, Americas, British Columbia, Canada, Connecticut, Northwest Territories, Puerto Rico, Trinidad and Tobago, Vancouver Island
A2h	Yes – Bahamas, Dominican Republic, Peru, Puerto Rico	Yes – Colombia, Cuba, New Mexico, Puerto Rico
A2h1	No	Yes – Argentina, California, Mexico, New Mexico, Puerto Rico, Western Canada, Western US
A2i	Yes – Ontario, Canada	Yes – Alberta, Canada, Colombia, Cuba, Manitoba, Massachusetts, Michigan, Nova Scotia, Ontario, Quebec, Saskatchewan, US, Wisconsin
A2j	No	Yes – Mexico, New Mexico
A2j1	No	Yes – Guatemala, Mexico, New Mexico, US

ML_AI

A2k	No	Yes – Ecuador, Mexico, Puerto Rico, Venezuela
A2k1	No	Yes – Colombia, Mexico, Puerto Rico, Peru, Venezuela
A2k1a	No	Yes – Peru, Puerto Rico, Trinidad and Tobago, Venezuela
A2l	No	Yes – Mexico, Texas, US
A2m	No	Yes – Argentina, Belize, Chile, Guatemala, Mexico, Southwest US, Texas
A2n	No	Yes – Alberta, Canada, Montana, Northern US, Quebec, Saskatchewan, Virginia, Wyoming
A2o	No	Yes – Mexico, Southwest US
A2p	Yes – British Columbia, Canada	Yes – Ecuador, Mexico, US
A2p1	No	Yes – Mexico
A2p2	No	Possibly – Mexico, uncertain
A2q	No	Yes – California, Chile, Colombia, El Salvador, Guatemala, Honduras, Mexico, US
A2q1	No	Yes – Arizona, California, Colorado, Mexico, US, Western US
A2r	No	Yes – Cuba, El Salvador, Guatemala, Kansas, Louisiana, Mexico, New Mexico
A2r1	No	Yes – Mexico, New Mexico, Kansas, US
A2s	No	Yes – Mexico
A2t	No	Yes – Mexico, Peru, US
A2-T16111C!	No	Yes – Brazil, Honduras, Louisiana, Mexico, Wyoming
A2-T16189C!	No	Yes – Brazil, Canada, Honduras, Louisiana, Mexico, Puerto Rico
A2u	No	Yes – South America, Colombia, Costa Rica, El Salvador, Guatemala, Mexico, Panama, Southwest US
A2u1	No	Yes – Mexico, US
A2u2	No	Yes – Colombia, Mexico, Panama, US
A2v	No	Yes – Colombia, Guatemala, Mexico, New Mexico, US

A2v1	No	Yes – Colorado, Guatemala, Mexico, New Mexico, US
A2v1a	No	Yes – Cuba, Guatemala, US
A2v1b	No	Yes – Guatemala, Mexico, New Mexico, US
A2v1-T152C!!!	No	Yes – Guatemala, Mexico, New Mexico, Texas, US
A2w	No	Yes – Caribbean, Cuba, Mexico, South America, US
A2w1	No	Yes – Cayman Islands, Colombia, Mexico, Panama
A2x	No	Yes – Mexico, Colombia, Kansas
A2y	No	Yes – Canada, Colombia, Colorado, Georgia, New Mexico, Peru, US
A2y1	No	Yes – Ecuador, Peru
A2z	Yes – Dominican Republic, Puerto Rico	Yes – Peru, Puerto Rico, US
A2z1	No	Yes – Peru, Puerto Rico
A2z2	No	Yes – Peru
A3	No	[133]Questionable – California
A5	No	Questionable – California
A6	No	Questionable – California
A7	No	Questionable – California
A8	No	Questionable – California
A9	No	Questionable – California
A10	No	Yes – California, Canada, Quebec, New York, Russia[134]
A11	No	Questionable – California
A12	No	Questionable – California
A13	No	Questionable – California

Please note that these are V17 haplogroup names, which will change with future mitochondrial haplotree versions. Please refer to "Native American Mitochondrial Haplogroups"[135] on DNAeXplain for current listings.

---

[133] These questionable haplogroups (A3, A5, A6, A7, A8, A9, A11, A12, A13) were reported in one paper where haplogroups A2, A3, A5, A6, A7, A9, A10 and A12 were reported to have been found among the Chumash Indians. Most of these haplogroups have not since been found as indigenous to the Americas.

[134] Haplogroup A10 is found in Asia, but is also found in the United States and in numerous places in Canada; it has been reported among the Chumash Indians as well.

[135] https://dna-explained.com/2013/09/18/native-american-mitochondrial-haplogroups/

Mitochondrial Native Haplogroup B

Ancient Mitochondrial Haplogroup B

Ancient haplogroup B, specifically B4 and subclades, is found in Mongolia and Tibet, and eastward into China, Taiwan, and Polynesia. Select subclades eventually migrated into the Americas. Haplogroup B4 is also found in Hungary, and B5 is found in Mongolia and Asia, but not in the Americas or Europe.

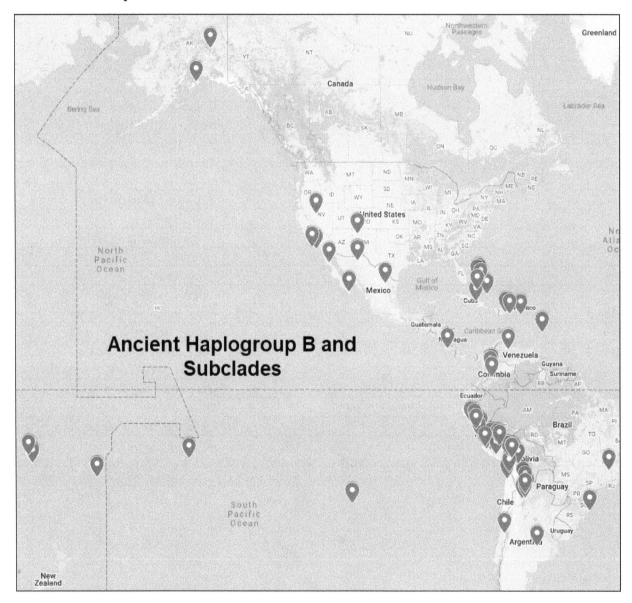

Haplogroup B is quite interesting.

The earliest ancient samples, all haplogroup B2 with no subclades noted, are found in Alaska dating from 12,000 years ago, but not in Canada or the eastern United States.

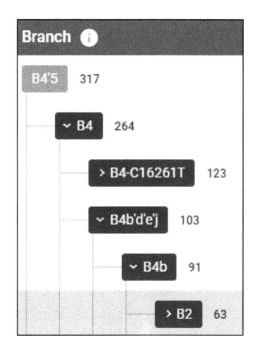

Haplogroup B2, with 63 downstream branches, is a subclade of haplogroup B4b.

The haplogroup B migration path is clearly coastal, traveling along the Pacific shore. People settled along the South American coast and into the Highlands of Peru, along with their haplogroup A family members.

The next oldest haplogroup B samples, dating from about 9,600 years ago, are found at the Lapa site in Brazil with the ancient haplogroup A samples. The Highlands of Peru aren't far behind though, with samples dating from about 8,500 years ago, and there are samples dating from 7,800 years ago from both Checua, Colombia,[136] and Pampas, Laguna Chica, Argentina.[137]

It's interesting to notice the pathway of several ancient samples dotting the Pacific. We know that the Hawaiian Islands were settled by Polynesian people. There's a pin on the easternmost island on this map, Easter Island. It's easy to mentally draw a line between Easter Island and the coast of South America. Indeed, there has been significant discussion about Polynesian admixture in the Native people, and vice versa, with some speculation that at least a few Native American people settled on Easter Island.

A paper written by Fehren-Schmitz et al. in 2017[138] laid that theory to rest, at least temporarily, with full sequencing of five pre-contact Easter Island samples focusing on admixture. The genomes of those individuals were entirely Polynesian, with no Native or other admixture. Their mitochondrial DNA fell into haplogroup B4a1a, B4a1a1, and B4a1a1m1, clearly Polynesian.

---

[136] https://en.wikipedia.org/wiki/Checua
[137] https://www.sciencedirect.com/science/article/pii/S2589004221005216
[138] https://www.sciencedirect.com/science/article/pii/S0960982217311946

However, a 2020 paper by Ioannidis et al.[139] and a 2021 paper by Willerslev suggests otherwise, stating that a faint Native signal is determined in Easter Island remains, but is believed to be from about the year 1300. Willerslev and Meltzer[140] suggest that perhaps Polynesian people did reach South America, and a few sailed west again, reaching Easter Island and possibly other locations as well. Perhaps additional testing of the aboriginal populations of South America, Australia, and New Zealand will help unravel this mystery. The jury is still out on this topic, which has tantalized researchers for years.[141]

In a paper written by Goncalves in 2013, a sample in a museum in Rio de Janeiro was misidentified as the extinct Botocundo Indians. Later, archival records dating from 1883/1884 in the Wellington (New Zealand) museum, now Te Papa, indicated that two Maori skulls were sent to Rio. Further analysis of the remains indicated that they were fully Polynesian, with no Native or other admixture. Their haplogroups were B4a1a1.[142] Unfortunately, this resulted in confusion and erroneous conclusions about South American Polynesian settlement.

Do we find ancient B4 in the Americas at all? Yes, there are two samples[143] in the Andes Mountains in northwest Argentina dating from between the years 1000 and 1450, pre-contact, one of which is found with two haplogroup B2 samples. This suggests that haplogroup B4 individuals migrated or at least lived with people who carried haplogroup B2 and subclades. These samples were only sequenced at the HVR1 level, or about 500 locations of the total 16,569 mitochondrial locations. If further sequencing is performed, the haplogroup B4 individuals would likely be assigned a subclade that would convey more information about their heritage.

The Andes Mountain range,[144] stretching from north to south along the entire continent of South America, provided caves and conditions conducive to preserving ancient remains. Remains in coastal areas or rainforests were more susceptible to deterioration.

How did those haplogroup B4 individuals come to be found with the Native people living in the Andes? Was haplogroup B4 found among the original settlers, or did B4 arrive with a later Pacific migration?

Is there any evidence of haplogroup B4a1 or subclades in the Americas today?

Yes, there is, but there's no concrete evidence that haplogroup B4a1 and its subclades are Native.

Haplogroup B4a1a1b is found in many locations, including the United States. According to the public FamilyTreeDNA mitochondrial tree, this haplogroup is found in the United States (9), Madagascar (5), Native American (4), South Africa (3), and India (1). The Genographic Project shows an additional three people in the United States who note that they are African American, plus one from Madagascar and one from Mauritius, an island about 1,000 miles east of

---

[139] https://www.nature.com/articles/s41586-020-2487-2?proof=t
[140] https://www.nature.com/articles/s41586-021-03499-y?proof=t
[141] https://www.idtdna.com/pages/community/blog/post/dna-links-prehistoric-polynesians-to-south-america
[142] https://dna-explained.com/2013/09/18/native-american-mitochondrial-haplogroups/
[143] https://revistas.unlp.edu.ar/raab/article/view/2459
[144] https://en.wikipedia.org/wiki/Andes

Madagascar. We know that enslaved people were imported from Madagascar, so we can't infer that haplogroup B4a1a1b is Native when there is matching and geographic information that tells us that B4a1a1b is found in other locations in the world.

B4a1a1a is found in Hawaii, but of course we know that Hawaii was settled by seafaring Polynesian people.

It's worth noting that B4a1 and subclades are not currently found in testers from the North American Pacific Coast region nor in South America along the coastline. If the Polynesians had continued their journey from Easter Island, they would have landed in South America along the Pacific Coast someplace. Even though it's tempting to draw that line between Easter Island and South America, there's no concrete evidence, at least not yet, that Polynesian sailors made it that far. More testers and research are needed.

Another interesting aspect of haplogroup B2, and specifically B2e, is that those are the only two haplogroups found on any of the Caribbean islands. It's certainly possible that some of the B2 samples, if they were fully sequenced, would also be haplogroup B2e. There are no other ancient samples of B2e, so it's possible that B2e originated in the Caribbean or on the mainland nearby.

Contemporary Mitochondrial Haplogroup B

Haplogroup B is widespread in the Americas. All of the haplogroup B found in the Americas today is either haplogroup B4'5, B2, or a subclade.

B4'5 is an example of a "joined" haplogroup. The apostrophe joining 4 and 5 means that in a previous version of the PhyloTree, haplogroups B4 and B5 were separate but were subsequently joined together into a master haplogroup above B4 and B5, with haplogroups B4 and B5 now individual subclade branches beneath B4'5. Rather than attempting to rename both entire branches, scientists combined the existing names into B4'5 as the parent. Today, the only people at FamilyTreeDNA placed at B4'5[145] are testers who have not completed a full sequence test. All others are able to be placed in a subgroup.

---

[145] https://www.familytreedna.com/public/mt-dna-haplotree/B;name=B4'5

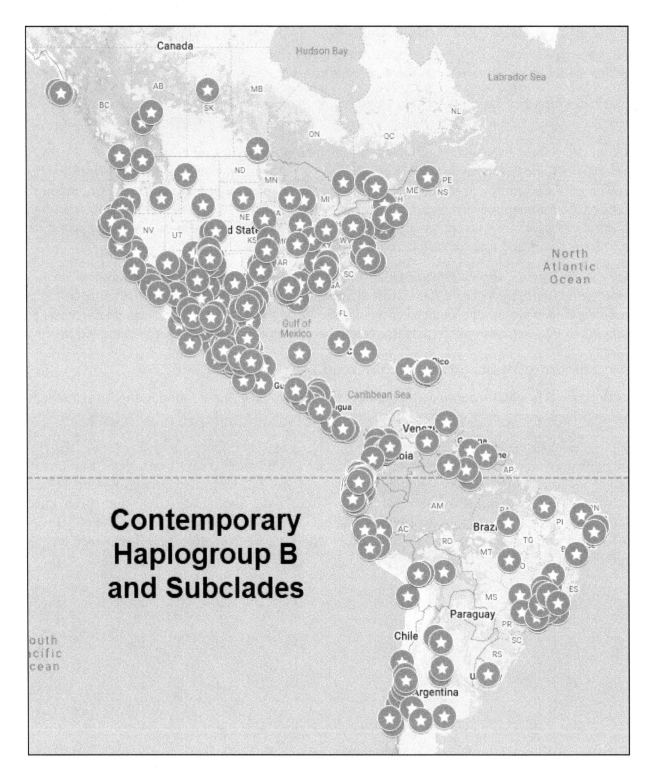

We find haplogroup B2 and many subclades throughout the Americas, with dense clusters found in Mexico and in the Arizona/New Mexico Reservation and Pueblo regions. Depending on the tribe or pueblo, Native people living in that region are either of Athabascan origin, having migrated around 600 years ago from present-day Alaska and Northwest Canada, or were the original inhabitants before being joined by the Athabascan people. The Navajo[146] and Apache[147] are both of Athabascan origin and migrated from the region of present-day Alaska. The Puebloan[148] were the original inhabitants of New Mexico and Arizona. These people are closely related to the people in Mexico.

Although separate reservations and pueblos exist today, many people are admixed with ancestors from throughout the region.

Haplogroup B Tribal Affiliations

We find haplogroup B and subclades among the following tribes:

Tribe	Haplogroup
Ache, Algonquian (New England), Arawak (Guyana and Suriname), Arikara Nation, Aymara/Inca (Chile), Caddo, Cherokee, Chickasaw, Coastal Pomo, Colville Confederated, Coreguaje, Gaviao, Guarani, Hidatsa, Huichol (Mexico), Karuk, Katuena, Mandan, Meskwaki/Sac and Fox of Mississippi in Iowa, Muscogee Creek, Quechua, Wuanana, Xavante, Yaqui	B2
Navajo	B2, B2b
Bella Coola, Chippewa, Cupeno (California), Houmas, Ojibwa, Kewa Pueblo people, Tsimshian, Yaqui (Mexico)	B2a
Chippewa/Ojibwa, Jemez Pueblo, Nahua (Mexico), Navajo	B2a1
Pecos Pueblo people	B2a1a
Mescalero Apache, Salinas Pueblo, Santa Anna Pueblo, Saulteaux First Nation Ojibwe (Alberta)	B2a2
Aztec (Mexico)	B2a3
Mayan (Guatemala), Santa Clara Pueblo	B2a4a
Hoopa, Pima, Tohono, O'Odham, Yuman	B2a5
Cayapa, Pomo, Shoshone-Bannock, Wailaki, Xavante	B2b
Shuar	B2b1
Apache, Beni	B2b2
Nomlaki, Yanomama	B2b3
Algonquian (Quebec), Carib (Trinidad and Tobago), Elsipogtog First Nations (New Brunswick, Canada), Kayapo	B2b3a

---

[146] https://en.wikipedia.org/wiki/Navajo

[147] https://en.wikipedia.org/wiki/Apache

[148] https://en.wikipedia.org/wiki/Puebloans

Ottawa, Passamaquoddy	B2c
Mixe	B2c1
Chibcha (Panama, Colombia), Chinandega, Guaymi/Ngobe (Panama), Wayuu	B2d
Yaqui	B2g1
Mesa Verde (Mexico)	B2g2
Waiwai	B2e
Ache	B2h
Kayapo	B2i1
Mapuche	B2i2a
Yaruro (Venezuela)	B2j
Wintu	B2l
Cherokee, Maidu, Maya	B2o
Huichol, Tewa	B2s
Mayan (El Salvador)	B2t
Andean Indian (Peru), Ho-Chunk	B2y
Chickasaw, Choctaw, Creek, Eastern Cherokee, Ho-Chunk Machapunga/Mattamsukeet, Pojoaque Pueblo, Zia Pueblo	[149]B4'5

Mitochondrial Haplogroup B -
Ancient and Modern Samples Found in the Americas

Haplogroup B is found throughout the Americas, although some subclades seem to be found exclusively in one region.

Haplogroup	Ancient	Modern
B	Yes – Peru	Yes – Mexico, US
B2	Yes – Alaska, Caribbean, Mexico, New Mexico, South America	Yes – Americas
B2a	Yes – Mexico	Yes – California, Canada, Ecuador, Guatemala, Louisiana, Mexico, New Mexico, Peru, US
B2aa	No	Yes – Ecuador, Mexico, Peru
B2aa1	Yes – Ecuador	Yes – Ecuador, Peru
B2aa1a	Yes – Peru	Yes – Peru
B2aa2	No	Yes – Mexico
B2ab	Yes – Bolivia, Peru	Yes – Peru
B2ab1	No	Yes – Peru
B2ab1a1	No	Yes – Peru

---

[149] Please note that haplogroup B4'5 is a very large base haplogroup that needs further breakdown and is found widely in Asia as well. B4'5 is a parent haplogroup of B2.

B2ac	No	Yes – Peru
B2ad	No	Yes – Peru
B2ae	No	Yes – Peru
B2ag	No	Yes – Peru
B2ag1	No	Yes – Peru
B2ah	No	Yes – Peru
B2a1	Yes – Nevada	Yes – Canada, Mexico, New Mexico, North Dakota, US
B2a1a	No	Yes – Arizona, California Mexico, New Mexico, Southwest US
B2a1a1	No	Yes – Arizona, Mexico, US
B2a1b	No	Yes – Canada, Colorado, Mexico, New Mexico, Ontario, Texas, US, Wyoming
B2a2	No	Yes – Alberta, Colorado, Mexico, New Mexico, Southwest US, Texas
B2a3	No	Yes – Mexico, New Mexico, US
B2a4	No	Yes – Mexico, New Mexico, US
B2a4a	No	Yes – California, Guatemala, Mexico, New Mexico, South Carolina
B2a4a1	No	Yes – Mexico, Southwest US, Texas
B2a5	Yes – California	Yes – Arizona, California, Mexico, New Mexico, Utah
B2a5a	Yes – Baja Mexico	No
B2a5b	Yes – California	No
B2b	Yes – Argentina, Bolivia, Peru	Yes – Idaho, Mexico, South America, Texas, US
B2b1	No	Yes – Ecuador, Peru, Venezuela
B2b2	No	Yes – Argentina, Bolivia, Honduras, Mexico, Texas, US
B2b2a	No	Yes – Bolivia, New Mexico
B2b3	No	Yes – Brazil, California, US, Venezuela
B2b3a	No	Yes – Brazil, Nova Scotia, Puerto Rico, Texas, Trinidad and Tobago, US, Venezuela
B2b4	No	Yes – Mexico, New Mexico
B2b5	No	Yes – Ecuador, Peru, Venezuela
B2b5a	No	Ecuador
B2b5a1	No	Yes – Ecuador
B2b5b	No	Yes – Ecuador

B2b5b1	No	Yes – Peru
B2b5b1a	No	Yes – Ecuador
B2b5b1a1	No	Yes – Ecuador
B2b6a	No	Yes – Ecuador
B2b6a1	No	Yes – Ecuador, Peru
B2b6a1a	No	Yes – Ecuador
B2b6a1a1	No	Yes – Ecuador
B2b6b	No	Yes – Ecuador
B2b6b1	No	Yes – Ecuador
B2b6b1a	No	Yes – Ecuador, Peru
B2b7	No	Yes – Ecuador
B2b8	No	Yes – Ecuador, Peru
B2b8a	No	Yes – Ecuador
B2b9	No	Yes – Ecuador, Peru
B2b9a	Yes – Peru	Yes – Peru
B2b9b	Yes – Peru	Yes – Peru
B2b9c	Yes – Peru	Yes – Ecuador, Peru
B2b10a	No	Yes – Peru
B2b10b	No	Yes – Peru
B2b11	Yes – Peru	Yes – Peru
B2b11a	Yes – Peru	No
B2b11a1	No	Yes – Peru
B2b11a1a	No	Yes – Peru
B2b11b	No	Yes – Peru
B2b11b1	No	Yes – Peru
B2b12a	No	Yes – Peru
B2b13	No	Yes – Peru
B2b-T152C!	No	Yes – Ecuador, Peru
B2c	No	Yes – Canada, Cuba, Ecuador, Maine, Mexico, Kentucky, Quebec, Texas, US, Washington
B2c1	No	Yes – Costa Rica, Mexico, US
B2c1a	No	Yes – Bolivia, Mexico, US
B2c1b	No	Yes – Mexico, US
B2c1c	No	Yes – Mexico, US
B2-C16278T!	No	Yes – Colorado, Honduras, Mexico, New Mexico, US
B2c2	No	Yes – Arizona, Bolivia, El Salvador, Guatemala, Mexico, New Mexico, US
B2c2a	Yes – Peru	Yes – Mexico, New Mexico, US
B2c2b	No	Yes – Arizona Mexico, New Mexico, US

B2d	Yes – Colombia, Costa Rica, Venezuela	Yes – Cuba, South America
B2e	Yes – Bahamas, St. Lucia	Yes – Argentina, Brazil, Colombia, Paraguay, Uruguay
B2f	No – Mexico	Yes – California, Chile, Mexico, New Mexico, Texas, US
B2g	No	Yes – Mexico, US
B2g1	Yes – Baja California	Yes – Arizona, California, Cuba, Mexico, US
B2g2	No	Yes – Mexico, Texas, US
B2h	No	Yes – Argentina, Brazil, Ecuador, Mexico, Montana
B2i2	No	Yes – Chile, Peru, US
B2i2a	No	Yes – Argentina, Chile, US
B2i2a1	No	Yes – Chile
B2i2a1a	No	Yes – Argentina, Chile, US
B2i2a1b	No	Yes – Argentina, Chile
B2i2b	Yes – Chile	Yes – Argentina, Bolivia, Chile, Peru
B2i2b1	No	Yes - Chile
B2j	Yes – Venezuela	Yes – Ecuador, Mexico, Peru, Venezuela
B2k	No	Yes – Mexico, Venezuela
B2l	Yes – Peru	Yes – Argentina, California, Chile, Ecuador Mexico, Texas, US, Venezuela
B2l1	No	Yes – Mexico
B2l1a	No	Yes – Ecuador
B2l1a1	No	Yes – Ecuador
B2m	No	Yes – Mexico, US
B2n	No	Yes – Mexico, New Mexico
B2o	Yes – Bolivia	Yes – Arizona, California, Canada, Colombia, Cuba, Georgia, Illinois, Louisiana, Mexico, New Mexico, South America
B2o1	No	Yes – Bolivia, Ecuador
B2o1a	No	Yes – Bolivia, Colombia, Peru
B2p	No	Yes – Mexico, Texas, US
B2q	No	Yes – Ecuador, Mexico, Peru
B2q1a	No	Yes – Ecuador, Peru
B2q1a1	No	Yes – Ecuador
B2q1b	Yes – Peru	Yes – Ecuador
B2r	No	Yes – Mexico, Panama
B2s	No	Yes – Mexico, New Mexico

113

B2t	No	Yes – Canada, El Salvador, Guatemala, Mexico, New Brunswick, New Mexico, US
B2u	No	Yes – Mexico
B2v	No	Yes – California, Mexico, New Mexico, Tennessee, US
B2w	No	Yes – Mexico
B2x	No	Yes – Mexico, Texas, US
B2y	No	Yes – Ecuador, Louisiana, Mexico, Peru, Wisconsin, US
B2y1	Yes – Chaco Canyon	Yes – Colorado, Mexico, New Mexico, US
B2y1a	Yes – California	No
B2y2	No	Yes – Peru
B2z	No	Yes – Ecuador
B2z1	No	Yes – Ecuador
B2z1a	No	Yes
B2-T16311C!	No	Yes – Mexico
B4	Yes – Argentina	Yes[150]
B4'5	No	Yes – Americas, but also some in other parts of the world[151]

Please note that these are V17 haplogroup names, which will change with future mitochondrial haplotree versions. Please refer to "Native American Mitochondrial Haplogroups" [152] on DNAeXplain for current listings.

Mitochondrial Native Haplogroup C

Ancient Mitochondrial Haplogroup C

Haplogroup C is found in Mongolia and the Baikal region, spread throughout most of central and eastern Asia, especially China, and into eastern Russia before crossing Beringia into the Americas. Like the other haplogroups, it is also found in Hungary.

Ancient haplogroup C is found less frequently in the Americas than haplogroups A or B. It does follow the same migration path, but there are just far fewer sites.

---

[150] B4 is likely a partial haplogroup given that B4, with no subgroups, is found only in Asia and Polynesia.
[151] Haplogroup B4'5 is a high-level haplogroup, the base of haplogroup B, and the root of B4. Most people assigned to haplogroup B4'5 need to order or upgrade to the full sequence test to receive a full haplogroup.
[152] https://dna-explained.com/2013/09/18/native-american-mitochondrial-haplogroups/

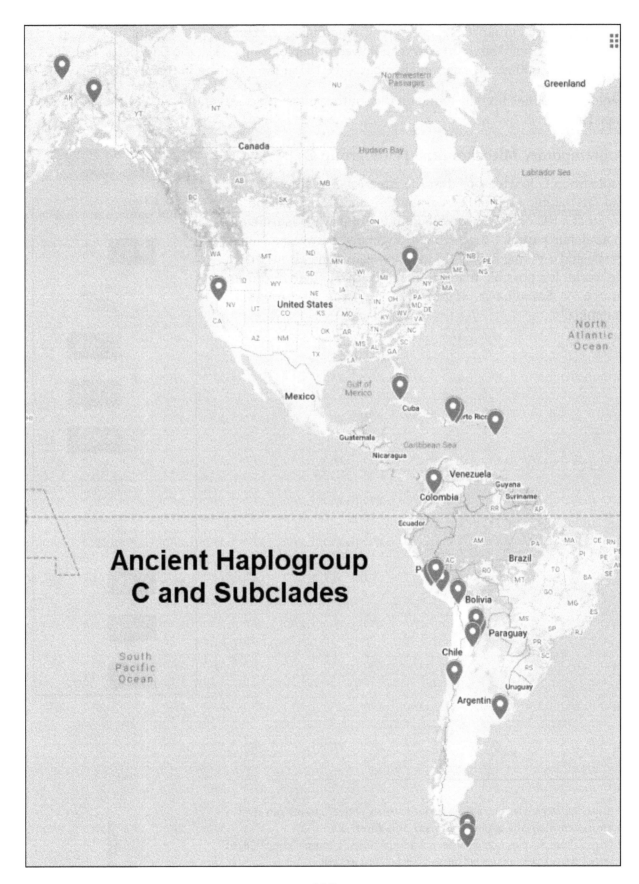

Ancient Haplogroup C and Subclades

The oldest Haplogroup C samples are haplogroup C1b, about 11,500 years old, found at the Upward Sun River[153] site[154] in Alaska, followed by haplogroup C1b at the Los Rieles, Los Vilos site in Chile at 11,000 years of age and haplogroup C1d1 at the Lapa site in Brazil at 10,000 years old.

Haplogroup C1b is literally found on the southernmost tip of Argentina, in a Mission cemetery at Cape Horn.

Contemporary Mitochondrial Haplogroup C

Haplogroup C is widespread in the Americas. Additionally, we find one sample each of haplogroup C1e and C1f in Iceland. In fact, that's the only C1e sample found, and it was identified in an academic paper,[155] suggesting it originated between a Native female and a Viking male. C1e has not been found elsewhere in the world. It's possible that C1e is not Native and arrived from Europe or Scandinavia. Haplogroup C1f was also found in Colombia.[156]

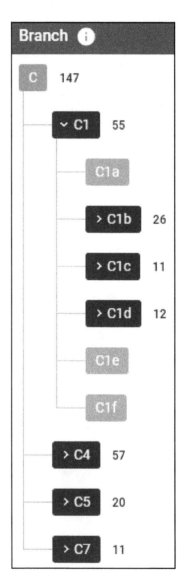

---

153 https://sites.google.com/a/alaska.edu/dr-ben-a-potter/upward-sun-river
154 https://en.wikipedia.org/wiki/Upward_Sun_River_site
155 https://journals.plos.org/plosone/article?id=10.1371/journal.pone.0087612
156 http://www.scielo.org.co/pdf/unsc/v20n2/v20n2a09.pdf

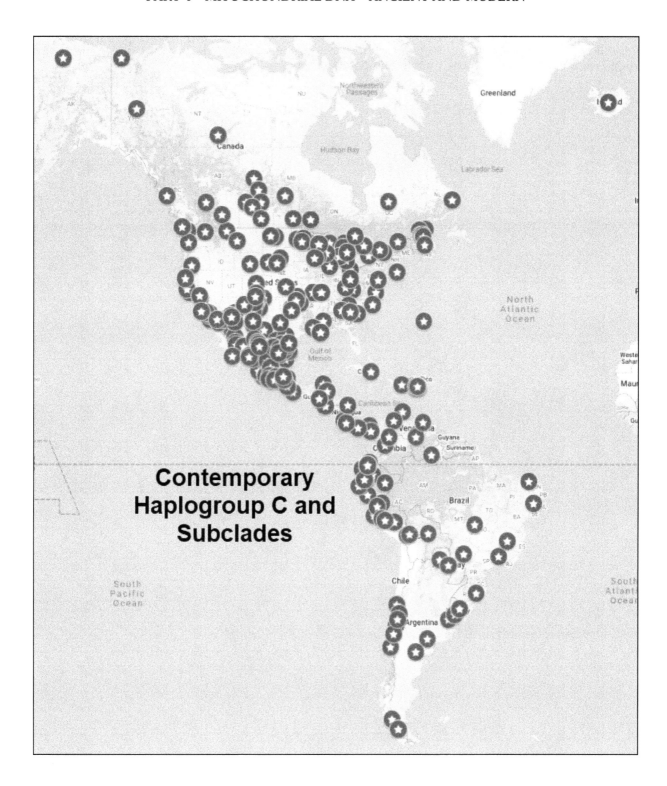

Contemporary Haplogroup C and Subclades

Haplogroup C shows a migration pattern similar to that of haplogroup B, with heavy clustering in Mexico and New Mexico in the pueblo and reservation areas.

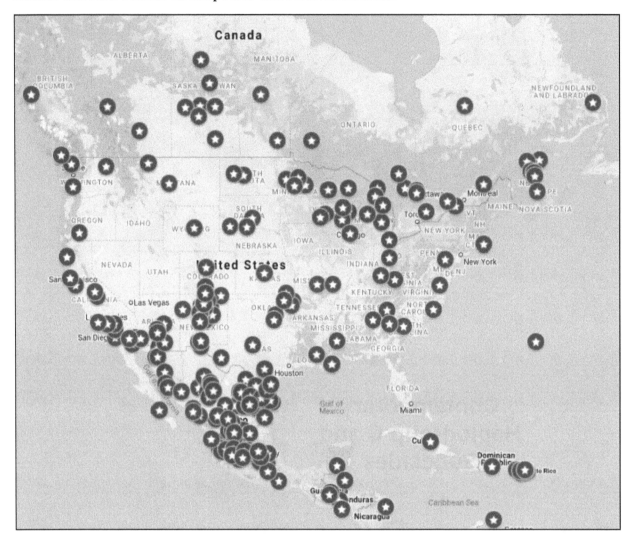

Haplogroup C is found in the Caribbean, but not widely distributed.

Haplogroup C Tribal Affiliations

We find haplogroup C and subclades among the following tribes:

Tribe	Haplogroup
Alacalufe (Chile), Algonquian, Anishinaabe, Apache, Arawak, Aztec (Mexico), Bari Motilon (Venezuela), Blackfeet from Montana, Blackfoot (Canada), Camba (Bolivia), Canada, Cherokee (East and West), Chickasaw, Chippewa, Choctaw, Chukchansi, Chumash, Cochini-Yuman, Cowlitz, Cree, Creek, First Nation of Nacho Nyak Dun (Yukon Territory), Halkomelem Salish, Hidatsa, Ho-Chunk, Hopi, Huron, Inca (Peru, Bolivia), Illinoise, Iroquois, Lakota Sioux, Lipan Apache, Luiseno, Mayan, Menominee, Mi'kmaq, Mixtec, Mohawk, Navajo, Odawa, Ojibwa, Otomi, Paiute, Pima, Potawatomie, Pueblo peoples, Quechua (Peru), Sault Ste Marie (MI) Tribe of Chippewa, Seneca, Shawnee, Shoshone, Taino, Tarahumara, Tarasco, Tongva, Yakui, Yakut (Russia), Yokut, Zapotec	C
Arawak, Hualapai, Pima	C1
Pima, Samish in British Columbia, Taino, (Puerto Rico), Wintu	C1b
Taino	C1b2
Rumsen	C1b7
Cherokee	C, C1c
Pima	C1c1a, C1c5
Mi'kmaq, Wintu	C1c6
Cree	C1d1a1
Chippewa, Inupiat	C4
Shuswap	C4c, C1d
Chippewa/Cree, Chippewa/Odawa (Michigan), Lakota, Mohawk, Shuswap	C4c1
Cherokee (East and West)	C4c1a
Lakota	C4c2

Mitochondrial Haplogroup C -
Ancient and Modern Samples Found in the Americas

The majority of haplogroup C in the Americas is haplogroup C1 and subclades, but we also find haplogroup C4 and subclades as well. We do find C2 in Mexico, but only in one 2007 academic paper.

Haplogroup	Ancient	Modern
C	Yes – Canada, Cuba, Mexico, South America	Yes – Caribbean, North and South America
C1	Yes – Arizona, California, Illinois, Nevada, South America	Yes – Argentina, Bolivia, Brazil, Canada, Chile, Mexico, Oregon
C1b	Yes – Alaska, California Mexico, Peru, St. Lucia, South America	Yes – Canada, Mexico, Michigan, New Mexico, Puerto Rico, South America, Virginia, Washington
C1b1	No	Yes – Mexico
C1b1a	No	Yes – Mexico
C1b1b	No	Yes – Mexico
C1bi	Yes – Inca Child Mummy in Argentina[157]	Yes – Mexico
C1b2	Yes – Caribbean	Yes – Cuba, Ecuador, Mexico, Peru, Puerto Rico
C1b2a	No	Yes – Peru
C1b2a1	No	Yes – Peru
C1b2b	No	Yes – Puerto Rico
C1b3	No	Yes – Argentina, Chile, Mexico, Peru, US
C1b4	Yes – St. Lucia	Yes – Mexico, Peru, Puerto Rico, US
C1b5	No	Yes – California, Mexico
C1b5a	No	Yes – Mexico, New Mexico
C1b5b	No	Yes – California, Mexico
C1b6	No	Yes – Argentina, Brazil
C1b7	No	Yes – California, Mexico
C1b7a	No	Yes – Mexico, US
C1b7a1	No	Yes – Mexico, US
C1b8	Yes – Argentina, Peru	Yes – Mexico
C1b8a	No	Yes – California, Mexico
C1b8a1	No	Yes – Mexico
C1b9	No	Yes – Mexico, US
C1b9a	No	Yes
C1b10	No	Yes – Mexico

[157] https://www.nature.com/articles/srep16462

C1b11	Yes – Mexico	Yes – Colombia, Mexico, Montana, New Mexico, Puerto Rico
C1b11a	No	Yes – Mexico
C1b11a1	No	Yes – Mexico, US
C1b11b1	No	Yes – Mexico, US
C1b12	No	Yes – Mexico
C1b12a	No	Yes – Mexico, US
C1b13	No	Yes – Argentina, Chile
C1b13a	No	Yes – Chile
C1b13a1	No	Yes – Chile
C1b13a1a	No	Yes – Chile
C1b13b	No	Yes – Chile
C1b13c	No	Yes – Chile
C1b13c1	No	Yes – Chile
C1b13c2	No	Yes – Argentina, Chile
C1b13d	No	Yes – Chile
C1b13e	No	Yes – Chile
C1b14	No	Yes – Mexico, US
C1b15	No	Yes – Peru
C1b15a	No	Yes – Brazil
C1b16	No	Yes – Peru
C1b17	No	Yes – Peru
C1b18	No	Yes – Peru
C1b19	No	Yes – Peru
C1b20	No	Yes – Peru
C1b21	No	Yes – Peru
C1b21a	No	Yes – Peru
C1b22	No	Yes – Peru
C1b23	No	Yes – Ecuador
C1b24	No	Yes – Peru
C1b25	No	Yes – Peru
C1b26a	No	Yes – Ecuador, Peru
C1b26a1	No	Yes – Peru
C1b27	No	Yes – Peru
C1b28	No	Yes – Ecuador
C1b40	Yes – Canada	No
C1b41a	Yes – Canada	No
C1b41a1	Yes – Canada, Mexico	No
C1b41a1a	Yes – Canada	No
C1b-T16311C!	Yes – Peru	Yes – Brazil, California, Canada, Mexico, New Mexico
C1c	Yes – Canada, Peru, Puerto Rico, South America, St. Lucia	Yes – Arizona, Canada, Cuba, Georgia, Mexico, New

		Brunswick, New Mexico, Puerto Rico, Quebec, Rhode Island, South America, South Dakota
C1c1	Yes – Bolivia, Mexico, Peru	Yes – California, Mexico, New Mexico
C1c1a	Yes – Mexico	Yes – Mexico, US
C1c1b	No	Yes – Mexico, US
C1c2	No	Yes – Cuba, Mexico, South Dakota, US
C1c4	Yes – Peru	Yes – El Salvador, Guatemala, Honduras, Mexico
C1c5	Yes – Mexico	Yes – Mexico, New Mexico
C1c6	No	Yes – California, Canada, Mexico, New Mexico, Newfoundland and Labrador
C1c7	No	Yes – Mexico, New Mexico, US
C1c8	Yes – Argentina	Yes – Wisconsin
C1c-T195C!	Yes – Curaçao	Yes – Mexico, New Mexico, Puerto Rico, US
C1d	Yes – Bahamas, Peru	Yes – Argentina, Canada, Colombia, Cuba, Mexico, New Mexico
C1d1	Yes – Brazil, Caribbean, Peru	Yes – Argentina, Cuba, Mexico, South America
C1d1a	No	Yes – Mexico, US
C1d1a1	Yes – Canada	Yes – Canada, Mexico, Montana, Oklahoma, Quebec, Saskatchewan
C1d1b	No	Yes – Argentina, Brazil, Chile, Paraguay, Peru
C1d1b1	No	Yes – Argentina
C1d1c	No	Yes – Mexico, US
C1d1c1	Yes – Cuba	Yes – Mexico, Michigan, New Mexico, Texas, Venezuela
C1d1d	No	Yes –Argentina, Brazil, Colombia, Ecuador, Uruguay
C1d1e	No	Yes – Argentina, Chile, Peru
C1d1f	No	Yes – Ecuador
C1d2	No	Yes – Colombia, Venezuela
C1d2a	No	Yes – Colombia
C1d3	No	Yes – Uruguay
C1d-C194T	No	Yes – Argentina, Columbia, Mexico, New Mexico
C1e	No	Yes – Iceland
C1f	No	Yes – Colombia

C2	No	Yes – Mexico
C4	No	Yes – Alaska, Minnesota, Russia
C4a	No	Yes – Siberia, US
C4c	No	Yes – North and South America (rare)
C4c1	Yes – Canada	Yes – British Columbia, Canada, Michigan, New Mexico, New York, Northwest Territories, Oklahoma, South Dakota
C4c1a	No	Yes – Canada, North Carolina, Oklahoma
C4c1b	No	Yes – North America
C4c2	No	Yes – Canada, New Mexico, South Dakota
CZ	Yes – Mexico	No

It is unclear whether C4 and C4a are Native. C4a is found in Asia among the Yakut people, as well as elsewhere. Haplogroup C4 may simply be a function of testing only at a high level. Time and more testers will provide additional information. C4c has one academic sample each in North and South America.

Haplogroup CZ is a base level haplogroup, the parent to both C and Z. It's likely that this sample was only sequenced to this very high level, or the researchers were only able to recover limited locations.

Please note that these are V17 haplogroup names, which will change with future mitochondrial haplotree versions. Please refer to "Native American Mitochondrial Haplogroups" [158] on DNAeXplain for current listings.

Mitochondrial Native Haplogroup D

Ancient Mitochondrial Haplogroup D

Ancient haplogroup D is found in the Baikal region of Asia. Some of the Tarim mummies[159] in China were found to be haplogroup D. Ancient haplogroup D is also found in Mongolia, Russia, and some samples from Hungary.

---

[158] https://dna-explained.com/2013/09/18/native-american-mitochondrial-haplogroups/
[159] https://en.wikipedia.org/wiki/Tarim_mummies

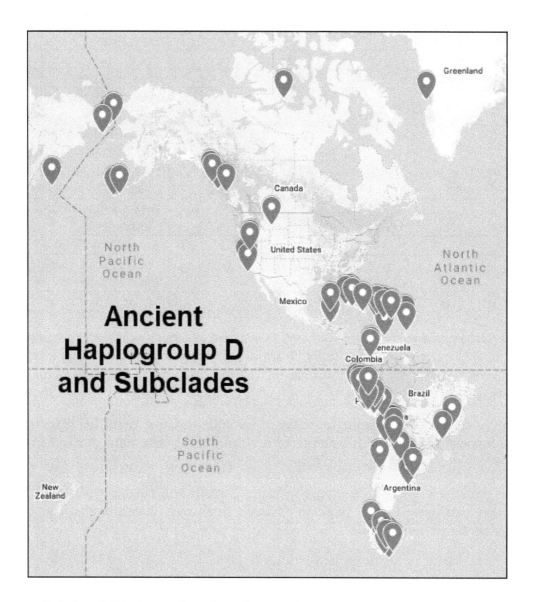

Haplogroups D1a1 and D2a1a are found on the Russian peninsula nearest Alaska, in Alaska and Canada, and in the Saqqaq sample in Greenland. This haplogroup appears to include Inuit individuals who are found in the circumpolar region.

Ancient haplogroup D has not yet been found in eastern Canada or the United States, other than along the Pacific coastline and in Montana.

The furthest eastern sample is the Anzick Child.[160] Anzick is also the oldest haplogroup D sample, dating from about 12,500 years ago, a member of the Clovis culture in Montana. Anzick's people apparently were part of a southern migration because his remains primarily match people in New Mexico, Mexico, and Central and South America, not people from Montana or contemporary northern tribes.

---

[160] https://en.wikipedia.org/wiki/Anzick-1

The next oldest haplogroup D remains are about 10,500 years old, found in On Your Knees Cave[161] on Prince of Wales Island in Alaska, followed by six samples found in a cave in Brazil.

The haplogroup D migration pattern appears to have been primarily along the Pacific Coast into South America. The Caribbean Islands were populated by South American peoples. Haplogroup D is also found in circumpolar populations.

Contemporary Mitochondrial Haplogroup D

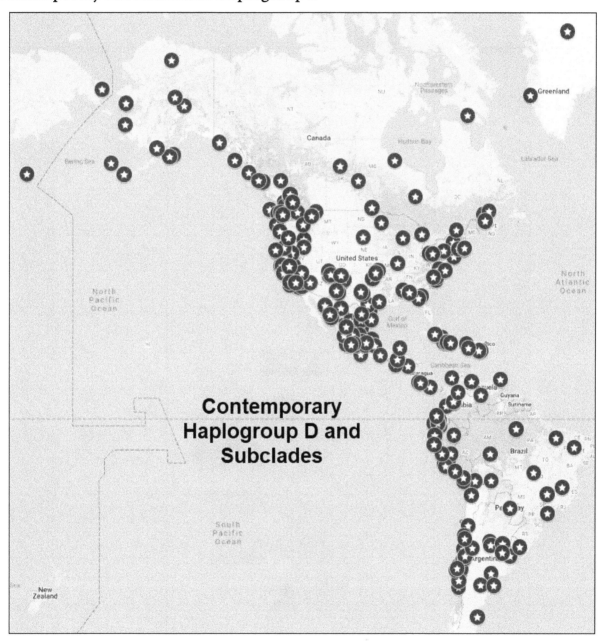

---

[161] https://en.wikipedia.org/wiki/On_Your_Knees_Cave

Contemporary haplogroup D is found in far eastern Russia on the Chukchi Peninsula and in the Commander Islands, throughout the Americas, and on Greenland. Haplogroup D indigenous samples fall primarily into subgroup D4, and in D1 and D2, both of which are subclades of D4.

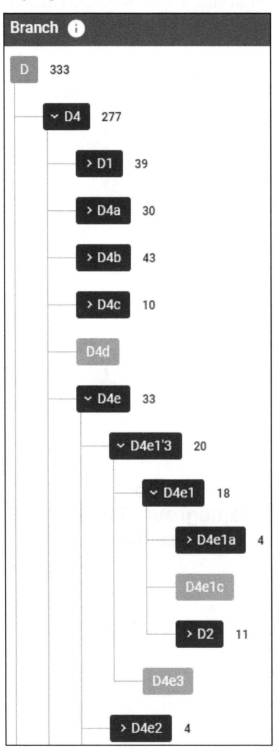

Haplogroup D Tribal Affiliations

We find haplogroup D and subclades among the following tribes:

Tribe	Haplogroup
Aleut, Apache, Athabascan, Aztec, Chemehuevi, Chinook Salish, Chippewa, Choctaw, Coast Miwok, Colville, Cora, Cree, Creek, Guarani, Haida, Huichol, Inca (Peru), Inuit (Greenland), Iroquois, Kahnawake Mohawk, Koyukon, Maidu, Mayan, Mescalero Apache, Miwuk, Moche (Peru), Mohawk, Na-dene, Nahuatl, Navajo, Nez Perce, Ohlone, Ojibwa, Osage, Pauite, Pequot, Piegan Tribe of Blackfeet, Popoluca, Quechua, Salish, Santa Inez Band Chumash, Seminole, Shoshone, Shuswap, Sugpiaq, Swampy Cree, Tewa, Thompson Salish, Tlingit Tsimshian, Yurok, Winnebago, Wintu	D
Anishnabe, Carib (Venezuela), Chumash, Coastal Salish Gabrielino, Haisla, Lenni Lenape, Miwok, Mi'kmaq, Mono, Narragansett, Ojibwa, Okanagan, Rumsen, Samish, Santa Ynez Band of Chumash, Tulalip, Yokuts, Yupik, Yurok	D1
Aleut	D1a1a1
Blackfoot (Canada)	D1d1
Apache	D1i2
Aleut, Inuit, Inupiat, Miwok, Tlingit	D2
Inuit, Inupiat, Na-Dene speakers	D2a
Inuit, Aleut Islanders	D2a1
Aleut	D2a1a
Navajo	D2a2
Inuit	D2a1b, D2a2, D2c, D3, D4b1a, D4b1a2a1
Chumash	D4, D7
Inupiat	D4b1a
Cahuilla	D5
Saami	D5a3a1a
Costanoan	D6
Vanyume	D8
Yokuts	D9
Salinan	D10

Mitochondrial Haplogroup D -
Ancient and Modern Samples Found in the Americas

Ancient haplogroup D is found in the Baikal region, Mongolia, China, and Russia as well as in North and South America and the Caribbean.

Haplogroup	Ancient	Modern
D	Yes – Peru	Yes – Caribbean, North and South America
D1	Yes – California, Caribbean, Nevada, South America	Yes – Caribbean, North and South America
D1a	No	Yes – Colombia, Commander Islands (Russia)
D1a1	Yes – Peru	Yes – Brazil
D1a1a1	No	Yes – Aleut
D1a2	No	Yes – Colombia
D1b	No	Yes – Mexico, Puerto Rico, Venezuela
D1c	No	Yes – Mexico, New Mexico
D1d	No	Yes – Mexico
D1d1	No	Yes – Canada, Ecuador, Mexico, Texas
D1d2	No	Yes – Mexico
D1f	Yes – Peru	Yes – Ecuador, Mexico, Peru
D1f1	No	Yes – Brazil, Colombia, Puerto Rico, Venezuela
D1f2	No	Yes – Brazil, Colombia, Venezuela
D1f3	No	Yes – California, Mexico, New Mexico
D1g	Yes – Argentina, Chile	Yes – Argentina, Brazil, Chile, Colombia, Mexico
D1g1	No	Yes – Argentina, California, Chile, Mexico
D1g1a	No	Yes – California, Chile, Mexico
D1g1a1	Yes – Ecuador	Yes
D1g2	No	Yes – Chile, Colombia
D1g2a	No	Yes – Chile
D1g3	No	Yes – Chile
D1g4	Yes – Argentina	Yes – Chile
D1g5	Yes – Argentina, Chile	Yes
D1g6	No	Yes – Chile
D1g-T16189C!	Yes – Argentina, Chile	Yes – Chile
D1h	No	Yes – Mexico
D1h1	No	Yes – California, Mexico
D1h2	No	Yes – Mexico
D1h3a8	No	Yes – Mexico

D1i	No	Yes – Mexico, New Mexico
D1i2	No	Yes – Mexico, New Mexico, Texas
D1j	No	Yes – Argentina
D1j1a	No	Yes – Argentina, Chile, Uruguay
D1j1a1	No	Yes – Chile, Argentina
D1k	No	Yes – Mexico, Texas
D1k1a	No	Yes – Peru
D1m	No	Yes – Mexico, New York, Cuba
D1n	No	Yes – Mexico
D1p	No	Yes – Peru
D1q	No	Yes – Peru
D1q1	No	Yes – Peru
D1r	No	Yes – Peru
D1r1	No	Yes – Peru
D1s	No	Yes – Peru
D1s1	No	Yes – Peru
D1t	Yes – Point Sal, California	Yes – Peru
D1u	No	Yes – Peru
D1u1	No	Yes – Peru
D2	Yes – North Slope Alaska	Yes – Aleut, California, Chukchi Peninsula (Russia), Commander Islands, Mexico, Pennsylvania
D2a	Yes – North Slope Alaska, Commander Islands	Yes – Alaska, Chukchi Peninsula (Russia), Na-Dene speakers
D2a1	Yes – Saqqaq sample in Greenland; Victoria Island, British Columbia	Yes – Alaska, Aleutian Islands
D2a1a	Yes – Alaska, Aleutian Islands	Yes – Alaska, Aleutian Islands, Commander Islands, Mexico
D2a2	No	Yes – Alaska, Arizona, Mexico, Siberia Chukchi Peninsula, US
D2b	No	Yes – Aleutian Islands, Chukchi Peninsula (Russia)
D2c	No	Yes – Alaska
D3	No (D3 sample was reclassified as D4b1a)	Yes – Alaska
D3a2a	No	Yes – Canada, Greenland
D4	Yes – Peru	Yes – California, Ecuador
D4b1a	Yes – Alaska North Slope	Yes
D4b1a2a1	Yes – Chukotka Peninsula, Peru, Russia	Yes – Alaska, Canada
D4b2a2	No	Yes
D4e1	No	Yes – Mexico
D4e1a1	No	Yes
D4e1c	No	Yes – Mexico

D4g1	No	Yes
D4h1a	No	Yes
D4h1a1	No	Yes
D4h1a2	No	Yes
D4h3	No	Yes – Mexico
D4h3a	Yes – Alaska, Argentina, Belize, Brazil, Chile, Colombia, Montana (Anzick Child), Peru	Yes – Argentina, Brazil, Chile, Colombia, Ecuador, Guatemala, Mexico, Peru
D4h3a1	No	Yes – Chile
D4h3a1a	No	Yes – Chile
D4h3a1a1	No	Yes – Chile
D4h3a2	No	Yes – Argentina
D4h3a3	No	Yes – Mexico, US
D4h3a3a	No	Yes – Mexico, US
D4h3a-C152T!!	No	Yes – Mexico
D4h3a4	No	Yes – Peru
D4h3a5	Yes – Argentina, Chile	Yes – Chile, Ecuador, Peru
D4h3a6	No	Yes – Colombia, Ecuador, Peru
D4h3a7	Yes – Alaska, British Columbia, Lucy Island (British Columbia)	Yes
D4h3a8	No	Yes – Mexico, Texas
D4h3a9	No	Yes – Peru
D4h3a11	No	Yes – Peru
D4h3a12	Yes – On Your Knees Cave, Alaska	No
D4h3a1a2	Yes – Chile	No
D4i2	No	Yes
D4j	No	Yes
D4j1a	Yes – Peru	No
D4j8	No	Yes – Argentina
D5	No	Yes – California
D5a2a	No	Yes

It is unclear whether haplogroup D5 and subclades are Native. D5 was identified in a 2008 academic paper, and no further information was provided about the D5a2a sample. Additional testing is needed.

Please note that these are V17 haplogroup names, which will change with future mitochondrial haplotree versions. Please refer to "Native American Mitochondrial Haplogroups" [162] on DNAeXplain for current listings.

---

[162] https://dna-explained.com/2013/09/18/native-american-mitochondrial-haplogroups/

Mitochondrial Native Haplogroup X

Ancient Mitochondrial Haplogroup X

The history of haplogroup X is less conclusive than haplogroups A, B, C, and D. Ancient haplogroup X is found in Mongolia, Hungary, and throughout Europe. The oldest non-Native ancient sample to date, X2b, is about 7,000 years old and was found in Austria.

The oldest Native sample is Kennewick Man, known as the "Ancient One" by Native Americans. Kennewick Man carries haplogroup X2a, is about 8,500 years old, and was found along the bank of the Columbia River in Kennewick, Washington.[163]

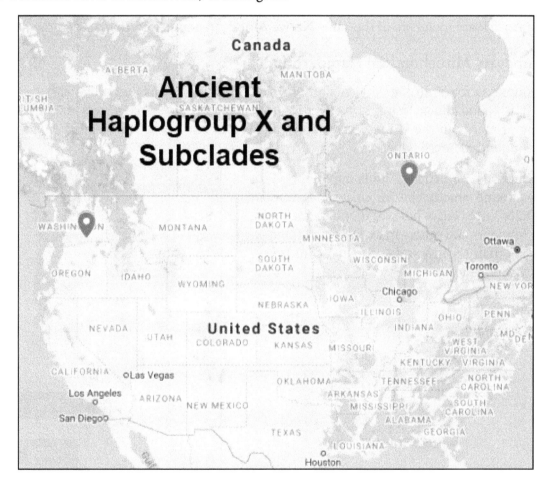

Only two ancient Native samples with haplogroup X have been discovered. Kennewick Man is haplogroup X2a, and a second sample from Ontario is haplogroup X2a1. The Ontario sample dates from between 1200-1300 CE, significantly after Kennewick Man, but pre-European contact.

---

[163] https://en.wikipedia.org/wiki/Kennewick_Man

Kennewick Man was controversial, as is haplogroup X more broadly. In the paper titled, "The ancestry and affiliations of Kennewick Man,"[164] published in 2015 by Rasmussen et al., the autosomal DNA of Kennewick Man was compared to worldwide populations.

Kennewick Man matches most closely with the Confederated Tribes of the Colville Reservation,[165] one of the five tribes who claim Kennewick Man as their ancestor. He is also closely related to the Ojibwa/Chippewa and Algonquian populations and shared a significant degree of ancestry with Native people from Central and South America. Kennewick Man matches these people more closely than people in populations anywhere else in the world, as does the Anzick Child, compared by the same authors.[166]

This analysis confirms that haplogroup X2a is indeed Native American and that both Kennewick Man and Anzick are members of the same Native American population that settled the Americas.

Contemporary Mitochondrial Haplogroup X

Haplogroup X is found in the Altai region of Asia and in the Evenks who live east of the Altai region. It is found much less frequently than the other Native haplogroups in the Americas, appearing primarily in the United States and Canada and one pocket in Mexico. A few samples have been found in South America.

Haplogroup X is a bit tricky. While haplogroup X2a is Native, found among the Mi'kmaq and Acadian people, X2b is not Native but was found in one of the Acadian founders and others in early French Canada. This means that it's easy to get the two confused—and many people do.

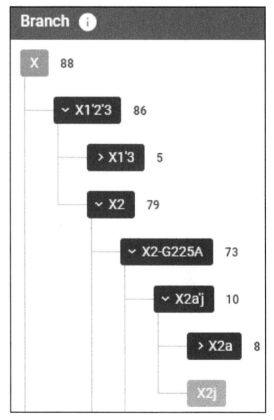

[164] https://www.nature.com/articles/nature14625
[165] https://en.wikipedia.org/wiki/Confederated_Tribes_of_the_Colville_Reservation
[166] https://www.nature.com/articles/nature14625

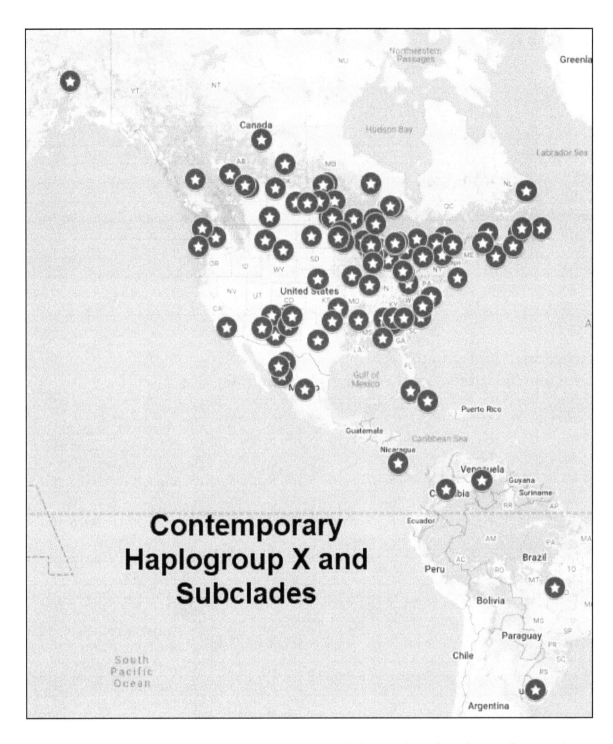

Unlike the other Native American haplogroups, X, excluding X2b, is found most frequently across the regions near the Canada/US border, suggesting these ancestors followed the water pathway of the Great Lakes and St. Lawrence River to Maritime Canada.

Haplogroup X Tribal Affiliations

We find haplogroup X and subclades among the following tribes:

Tribe	Haplogroup
Algonquian, Cree, Ho-Chunk, Mi'kmaq, Navajo, Nuu-chah-nulth, Sioux, Yakama	X
Chippewa, Ojibwa	X2a1
Sioux	X2a1a
Jemez Pueblo, Sioux	X2a1a1
Chippewa/Ojibwa	X2a1b
Chippewa	X2a1b1a, X2a1c
Navajo	X2a2
Ojibwa	X2g
Huichol, Taramahura	X6
Yanomani	X7

Mitochondrial Haplogroup X -
Ancient and Modern Samples Found in the Americas

Haplogroup	Ancient	Modern
X	No	Yes – Manitoba, Maryland, Mexico, Newfoundland and Labrador, Nova Scotia, Ontario, Wisconsin
X2	No	Yes
X2a	Yes – Kennewick Man, Washington	Yes – California, Canada, Cuba, Manitoba, Mexico, Newfoundland, Ontario, Saskatchewan
X2a1	Yes, Lucier in Southwest, Ontario	Yes – Canada, Manitoba, Manitoulin Island on the US/Canada border, Montana, New York, Oklahoma, Virginia, Wisconsin
X2a1a	No	Yes – Manitoba, US
X2a1a1	No	Yes – New Mexico
X2a1b	No	Yes – Alberta, Manitoba, New Mexico, Ontario, Rhode Island
X2a1b1a	No	Yes – Manitoba
X2a1c	No	Yes – Michigan, Wisconsin
X2a2	No	Yes – Newfoundland and Labrador, New Mexico, Nova Scotia, Quebec

X2g	No	Yes – Great Lakes Region, Michigan
X6	No	Mexico
X7	No	Brazil, Venezuela

Some haplogroups, such as X2g, X6, and X7 are exceedingly rare. X2g is found only in the Great Lakes area and Michigan. X6 is found in three Mexican samples, two of which are among the Huichol and Tarahumara people. X7 is only found in two samples, in Venezuela and Brazil.

Please note that these are V17 haplogroup names, which will change with future mitochondrial haplotree versions. Please refer to "Native American Mitochondrial Haplogroups" [167] on DNAeXplain for current listings.

Haplogroup X2b

Haplogroup X2b and subclades are missing from this list because X2b is clearly European, not Native. In early testing, before full sequencing was available or popular, genealogists interpreted haplogroup X to mean Native, which is not always the case.

Acadian families who founded a colony on Nova Scotia in the early 1600s did intermarry with the Native people, some of whom do carry indigenous subclades of haplogroup X, so the misinterpretation was easy to understand.

Because Radegonde Lambert, one of the early Acadians, carried haplogroup X2b4, and the Acadians were known to have intermarried with the Mi'kmaq, haplogroup X2b4 was "assigned" as Native among genealogists. Radegonde's unidentified mother had already been speculated to be Native American, in part because she could not be identified. Keep in mind that the less complete tests—such as haplogroup-only tests or the HVR1/HVR1 regions of the mitochondrial DNA, which used to be the entry-level mitochondrial test—only returned either haplogroup X or X2. As mentioned earlier, X2a, which is one branch of X2, is Native, but X2b is not.

As additional people were tested and other X2b4 individuals from European countries were identified, [168] it became obvious that Radegonde's mother was not Native, [169] but instead an unidentified European woman. While my analysis was not popular in 2016, [170] testing since has confirmed those results and now, in most cases, the genealogy of Radegonde's maternal origins has been corrected.

---

[167] https://dna-explained.com/2013/09/18/native-american-mitochondrial-haplogroups/

[168] https://www.familytreedna.com/public/x?iframe=mtresults

[169] https://dna-explained.com/2016/09/14/haplogroup-x2b4-is-european-not-native-american/

[170] https://dna-explained.com/2016/09/18/radegonde-lambert-16211629-16861693-european-not-native-52-ancestors-132/

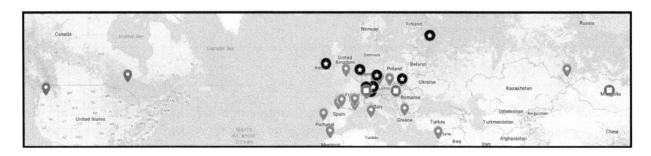

This map shows only ancient DNA where haplogroup X2a is found in the Americas, but haplogroups X2b (pin), X2b4 (circle with star), and X2b4a (circle with square) are found only in Europe.

"Unknown" does not equal Native American, an error that too often occurs in genealogy. Fortunately, we have mitochondrial DNA to either confirm or refute matrilineal Native heritage.

Mitochondrial Outlier Haplogroups

Two small subclades of other haplogroups have been found in circumstances that suggest they may be Native. If you're noticing my carefully worded speculation, you're probably laughing. I do not want to be the person who fuels unfounded rumors or misinformation. On the other hand, theories that await enough evidence to be considered proof, or enough negative evidence to disprove the theory so it can be dismissed, are the foundation of scientific endeavor. Therefore, I'm sharing this information, but this is absolutely not proven and needs to be considered a speculative theory that is under consideration.

Haplogroups F1a1 and F1a1a

Haplogroup F1a1a may be an indigenous haplogroup, or more properly stated, F1a1a may have an indigenous subgroup yet to be defined.

Slowly over the years, more testers who carry haplogroup F1a1 and F1a1a have identified as Native American or Mexican. Between 85–90% of Mexican people carry Native American mitochondrial DNA.

When assigning a haplogroup as Native American, several factors are taken into consideration:

- Is the haplogroup directly above this one in the tree identified/proven as Native?

- Are multiple other people in this haplogroup Native?

- Are people tribally affiliated, not just repeating oral history?

- Are multiple other people in this haplogroup positively not native and not born in a location that can be confused with Native? For example, not "US," not "Canada," and not "Spain," which is the ancestral location entered by many Hispanic people.

- If some people in the haplogroup are not Native, are there defining mutation groups between those who are not Native and those who identify as Native that separate the two groups?

- Are we seeing one-off, singleton identifications that could be either a misunderstanding of the instructions, confusion about a matrilineal ancestral line, or an unknown historical genealogical event?

- Are we seeing geographic clusters of this haplogroup? Is there a historical event that could explain this haplogroup in a location that is not Native. Haplogroup X2b4 found in Acadian descendants from Nova Scotia is a good example.

Of course, we may not be able to answer all these questions for each candidate haplogroup. We must work with the information we have at hand.

Haplogroup F1a1a is found in a cluster in Mexico, with at least one ancestor documented back into the 1870s.

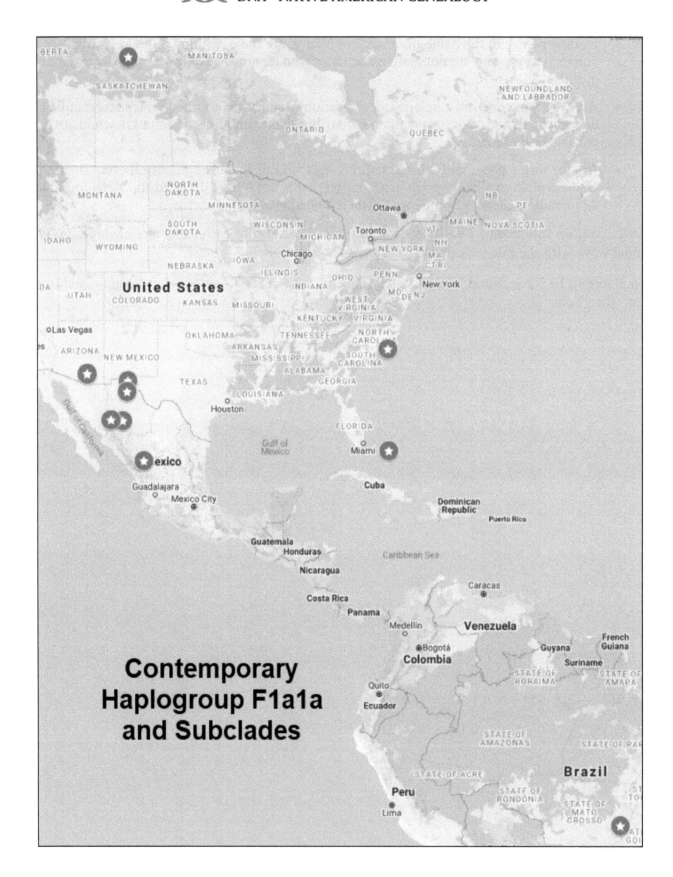

Contemporary Haplogroup F1a1a and Subclades

There are no haplogroup F1a1a or F1a1 ancient remains in the Americas. Haplogroup F1a1a is typically found in Asia and Polynesia as is its parent group, F1a1, and its subgroup, F1a1a1.

However, there is a cluster of several F1a1a people found in northern Mexico and just across the border in New Mexico and Arizona. Three F1a1 individuals are also found in Mexico. Additionally, we find a few single F1a1a identifications in various other locations. Note that the Canadian individual is likely from Eastern Canada, but I can't confirm that, so the pin is located in the middle of Canada.

Whether haplogroups F1a1 and F1a1a are indigenous remains to be proven. Regardless, one way or another, females with Asian/Polynesian haplogroups F1a1 and F1a1a somehow settled in the northwest portion of Mexico. How that happened may actually be the story to be told.

Once again, more testing is needed.

Haplogroup M

Haplogroup M has been confounding researchers for years. In 2007 Malhi et al. reported that haplogroup M was discovered in ancient DNA in China Lake, British Columbia, dating from about 5,000 years ago.[171] This discovery was reported again in a 2013 paper that Malhi co-authored, Cui et al., which stated that those two individuals from the same burial site form a macrohaplogroup of M that has yet to be identified in contemporary Native people.[172] Note that the mitochondrial DNA from other burials at this site do correlate to known Native haplogroups found in current populations. This suggests that either this lineage was misidentified or eventually became extinct, or the line still exists, is vanishingly rare, and the right people just haven't tested yet.

Recent analysis has revealed numerous individuals indicating Native ancestry with various haplogroup M subclades, but none sufficiently convincing to stand alone, meaning no tribal affiliation was provided, nor were clusters of people discovered. Furthermore, these people did not all fall into the same haplogroup M subclade, but instead individually in many subclades.

Confusing the situation further, we know that haplogroup M is found sporadically in continental Africa and on the island nation of Madagascar off the east coast of Africa. Some enslaved people were imported from this region during slave trading, which means that haplogroup M could be found in people who identify as Native and are also mixed African. In fact, several individuals identified themselves as either mixed Native/African American or African American. The only geographically common factor was that several people listed their matrilineal ancestor's location in a southeastern state.

Without direct documentary evidence of their associated genealogy as Native or finding haplogroup M among Native people in other portions of the United States and Canada, such as in proximity to the China Lake site, we can't assume that the haplogroup M descends from a Native

---

[171] https://www.sciencedirect.com/science/article/abs/pii/S0305440306001488
[172] https://www.ncbi.nlm.nih.gov/pmc/articles/PMC3700925/

ancestor. Furthermore, the lack of consistency in haplogroup assignments suggests alternative scenarios for why some haplogroup M individuals note themselves as Native American.

I found the following examples:

- More than 25 people identifying as Native or Native mixed with another ethnicity, all originating in the southeast United States.

- Three people who identify as Cherokee. Unfortunately, Cherokee is often used as a generic word (like "Kleenex") when an actual tribe is unknown. Only one individual's earliest known ancestor was from a location associated with the Cherokee.

- Several people from both Canada and Mexico who did not provide any ethnicity. Based on their surnames, some were almost assuredly born in Asia. One appears to be Acadian and does claim Native heritage.

- Scattered individuals from Latin and South America, with only a couple claiming indigenous heritage.

Unfortunately, these individuals span many subclades of haplogroup M, making a definitive argument for haplogroup M being one of the founding Native American haplogroups all but impossible at the present time. Our best piece of evidence remains the China Lake ancient samples.

Furthermore, East Indian[173] people, under British rule, were transported as indentured servants to the Caribbean,[174] Guyana, [175] and southern colonial plantations.[176] Haplogroup M is common among people from India.

Without additional evidence, we cannot yet draw any conclusions about finding haplogroup M in the Americas in present-day testers, although based on the information we do have, it looks doubtful.

---

[173] https://en.wikipedia.org/wiki/East_Indies
[174] https://www.jstor.org/stable/27866418
[175] https://www.historytoday.com/archive/guyanese-slaves-india-caribbean
[176] https://digitalcommons.lsu.edu/cgi/viewcontent.cgi?article=2611&context=gradschool_disstheses

PART 5

Y DNA – ANCIENT *and* MODERN

Indigenous American Y DNA

Y DNA Haplogroup Formation

Y DNA haplogroups can be traced back to a man affectionately known as Y-line Adam or Y-Adam, who lived approximately 230,000 years ago in Africa.

Native American Y DNA haplogroups fall into two base haplogroups, Q and C, with haplogroup Q being substantially more widespread than haplogroup C. As with mitochondrial haplogroups, only some subclades of Q and C are Native.

FamilyTreeDNA maintains a free public Y DNA haplotree.[177] The Y DNA tree is handled differently than the mitochondrial DNA tree. While only full sequence mitochondrial DNA tests are included in the mitochondrial DNA tree, Y DNA tests that have either various levels of partial or advanced SNP tests are included in the Y tree:

- The Big Y

- Big Y-500

- Big Y-700

- Single, individual SNP tests

- SNP packs that confirm a group of SNPs for a specific haplogroup

In other words, if the men who purchased SNPs upgraded to the most granular Big Y test, their haplogroup would very likely change and they would be placed further down on the tree. This would, in essence, shift their earliest known ancestor's geographic location information from their current haplogroup to their new, much more specific haplogroup.

SNPs are the same kind of nucleotides found in mitochondrial DNA that mutate from T, A, C, or G to a different nucleotide. However, Y DNA also includes an additional type of repeat mutation that is tested in the 12–111 panels and includes up to 700 total STR (short tandem repeat) values in the Big Y-700 test.[178] While SNPs are a change at one location, STR values are like a copy error where a group of SNPs get repeated and inserted several times.

---

[177] https://www.familytreedna.com/public/y-dna-haplotree/A
[178] https://dna-explained.com/2014/02/10/strs-vs-snps-multiple-dna-personalities/

PANEL 1 (1-12)					
Marker	DYS393	DYS390	DYS19**	DYS391	DYS385
Value	13	24	15	11	11-14

Men can purchase STR tests to match other testers at an introductory level, and the results are shown in panels. An example of the first 5 STR values in Panel 1 (markers 1–12) is shown above. STR tests are sold as 37 and 111 marker tests. The Big Y "Explorer" test includes a minimum of 700 STRs (including the original 111), along with sequencing of the majority of the Y chromosome for haplogroup assignment.

STR marker values are shown with a value that represents the number of copy insertions. At location DYS393, this man has 13 copies. FamilyTreeDNA matches these values to other testers looking for match patterns.

Anyone who takes an STR test, meaning a 12–111 marker test, but not a Big Y test receives an estimated high-level haplogroup based on those STR values. Native American men in haplogroup Q often receive an estimated haplogroup of Q-M3, and haplogroup C Native American men receive an estimated haplogroup of C-P39.

The only way to verify these haplogroups and extend them downstream to subgroups is to do one of the following:

- Purchase an individual SNP test, which only tests one specific SNP location

- Purchase a SNP pack, which tests roughly 100 SNPs in order to verify a partial path down the haplogroup tree

- Purchase the Big Y-700 test, which tests the gold standard region of the entire Y chromosome and is the recommended purchase

The results of all three types of SNP verification are important and are therefore included on the tree—but you can't assume that a man included on a higher Q branch, such as haplogroup Q-M242, is only haplogroup Q-M242 and not a subgroup. He may not have tested at the Big Y-700 level. He may have taken an earlier Big Y-500 test and not upgraded.

Searching by country on the FamilyTreeDNA public tree for "United States (Native American)" within haplogroup Q shows the following haplogroups:

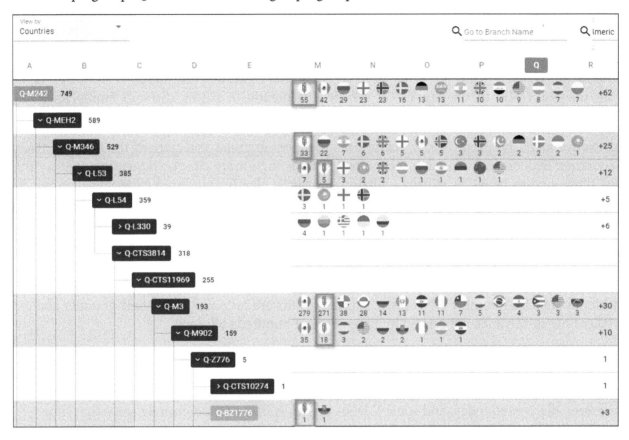

Looking at the Native feather flags in the first three gray, selected haplogroups, we see that while there are many Native people, there are also many listed in those haplogroups who are not Native. This suggests that many of these men took a confirming SNP test, but not the full Big Y-700 test. If they took the Big Y test, they would either discover that they belong on a Native or non-Native branch, removing any ambiguity.

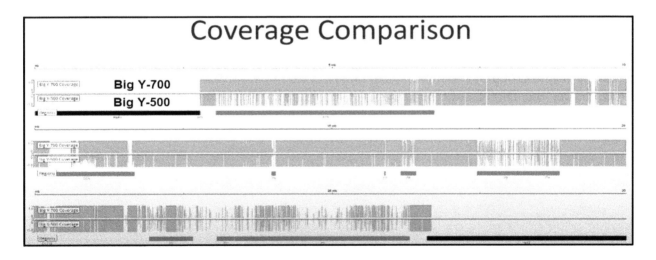

The bottom image on page 143, courtesy of FamilyTreeDNA, shows that the Big Y-700 test, shown as the top bar, increased the high-quality read coverage of the Y chromosome by approximately 50%, dramatically increasing the ability to determine novel branching required for haplogroup discovery. In other words, the Big Y-700 test is far more useful in deciphering how multiple men descend from common ancestors, both historically and in a genealogical time frame.

Additionally, most—if not all—men have received more granular haplogroups after upgrading from the Big Y-500 to the Big Y-700, which aids greatly in sifting through family lines and determining who is descended from whom.

For Native men, the Big Y-700, which utilizes the most granular and state-of-the art NGS (Next Generation Sequencing) scanning technology, groups men more closely; hopefully, one day this will allow men to be either tribally affiliated or at least clearly associated by language group. In some cases, this is already happening when mutations are only found among members of a specific tribe or family.

Y DNA Academic Sampling and Consumer Testing

The good news is that with the scientific advancements being continuously introduced and refined by FamilyTreeDNA in the Y DNA testing space, results are becoming extremely granular and can predict how closely men are related in increments of hundreds of years.

The bad news is that academic samples are not processed in university labs using this technology, so the results can be challenging to compare. The Genographic Project only tested selected locations to identify SNPs associated with a particular branch of the Y DNA tree. Many more SNPs have been discovered today, and some Y DNA branches have shifted entirely since that time.

Early Y DNA samples were processed using only the highest level of Y DNA SNP testing, providing only high-level haplogroups. This was sufficient to identify the samples as Native, as opposed to European or Asian, but not sufficient to identify the samples more granularly beyond that. Most of the academic samples are only classified to either Q-M3 or Q-M242.

Early Genographic samples were only reported to the Q-M242 level, which is the base haplogroup for Q. This provides no ability to differentiate between Native and non-Native samples. Genographic 2.0 samples did provide somewhat more specific differentiation, with Native samples assigned to Q-M3.

This wide variety of haplogroup testing methodologies, including selective SNP testing, makes creating a "Haplogroup by Location" chart, like I did for mitochondrial DNA, virtually impossible. Furthermore, the list of subgroups beneath haplogroup Q-M3 and Q-Z780, the indigenous subgroups, currently stands at 261, making the list long and untenable.

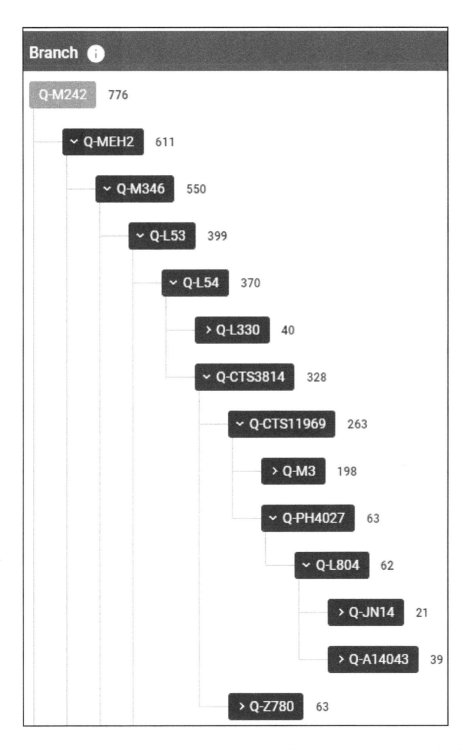

Not all subgroups of Q-M3 and Q-Z780 are Native.

The haplogroup Q and haplogroup C maps provide a great deal of information. More recent whole genome sequencing by independent labs has been introduced into the mix as well. Whole genome testing does sequence the entire genome, but several challenges have yet to be overcome, both for ancient and contemporary DNA samples.

Challenges in whole genome sequencing of ancient remains include the following:

- Fragmented DNA results not allowing detailed interpretation of Y DNA results
- Low-coverage reads that do not facilitate detailed and granular haplogroup assignments
- The necessity to be performed in specialized "ancient DNA" labs

Low-cost whole genome testing for direct consumers generally only scans each location a few times, whereas Big Y testing scans a minimum of 30 times. Additionally, special enrichment techniques developed for the Big Y test allow the Big Y to reliably sequence areas not previously accessible, as described in the Big Y-700 white paper.[179]

Whole genome sequencing does not return Y DNA, mitochondrial DNA, or autosomal files separately, nor do those vendors provide matching. Consumers must figure out how to extract their Y DNA information and have no access to the matching database at FamilyTreeDNA. In time, high-quality whole genome sequencing will be convenient and affordable for consumers, but that day has not arrived just yet.

Haplogroup Naming Conventions

Mitochondrial DNA Haplogroups

When mitochondrial DNA samples have been fully sequenced, we can conclusively assign a haplogroup based on the standardized tree in effect at the time of sequencing.

As the PhyloTree evolves and changes, branches are added, shuffled, and deleted. While FamilyTreeDNA reassigns customer haplogroups based on the current tree, that doesn't happen with academic samples. The old assignments stay in place with no avenue for updating the results to new haplogroups. One would think that, with today's automation capability, an innovative graduate student who needs a Ph.D. project would see the opportunity and fulfill this need.

Y DNA Haplogroups

Y DNA haplogroup names have evolved and are handled differently than mitochondrial DNA haplogroups, although they both began with a simple letter + number system. Today, Y DNA haplogroup names are assigned by SNP name, not by a letter + number system.

For example, the "old" letter + number system equated haplogroup Q-M3 to Q1a1a1a1. As new branches were discovered, existing branches either had a new letter or number appended, or the entire branch was shifted, grafted, and renamed entirely. Over time, this methodology became impossible to maintain, and haplogroup letter/number names became in excess of 20 characters long. However, the older names remain in earlier publications. Unfortunately, without knowing which "tree" was in effect at the time, there's no way to know what the SNP equivalent to Q1a1a was back when a paper was published.

---

[179] https://blog.familytreedna.com/wp-content/uploads/2018/06/big_y_700_white_paper_compressed.pdf; The Y chromosome contains approximately 57 million nucleotides, not all of which are available for sequencing for a variety of scientific reasons, reducing the accessible areas to about 23.5 million. The Big Y-700 successfully reads about 22.5 of those 23.5 million locations.

The volunteer organization ISOGG began maintaining Y DNA equivalence trees in 2006, providing a translation service between the letter/number and SNP naming systems.[180] Today, the letter number system is only used or referenced for very high-level conversational haplogroup assignments.

At FamilyTreeDNA, new Y DNA haplogroups are literally discovered daily. Its tree is updated nightly, reflecting branch splits and newly discovered haplogroups.

As of July 2021, the Y DNA tree had just under 47,000 branches (plus equivalent branches just waiting to be split), while the mitochondrial DNA tree V17, much more static in nature, had 5,433 branches. The mitochondrial tree won't receive additions until the Million Mito Project releases an update, but the Y DNA tree grows daily and by thousands of branches every year.

Y DNA Native Haplogroup Q

Not all subclades of haplogroup Q are Native. Subclades of haplogroup Q are found throughout Europe, including in Scandinavia and parts of Asia. A few instances of haplogroup Q have been found in the Near East, and one branch of Q is found in the Jewish population.

Ancient Y DNA Native Haplogroup Q

The oldest haplogroup Q sample dates from about 15,000 years ago from the Altai region[181] of Russia.[182] Other ancient samples are found in the Baikal region, Mongolia, and throughout Siberia, including the Chukotka Peninsula in far eastern Siberia—the gateway to Beringia. We also find ancient haplogroup Q extending westward into Hungary and north into Scandinavia.

The oldest Native American sample is the Anzick Child,[183] a Clovis burial dating from about 12,500 years ago in what is now western Montana. The next oldest North American samples are from Spirit Cave in Nevada[184] and On Your Knees Cave[185] in Southwestern Alaska, from about 10,500 years ago.

One sample in Chile dates from about 11,000 years ago, and samples from Brazil and Argentina aren't far behind. The Native people traversed a great distance in a relatively short time after their arrival on the American continents.

---

[180] https://isogg.org/tree/
[181] https://en.wikipedia.org/wiki/Afontova_Gora
[182] https://www.sciencedirect.com/science/article/abs/pii/S1068797117300044
[183] https://en.wikipedia.org/wiki/Anzick-1
[184] https://en.wikipedia.org/wiki/Spirit_Cave_mummy
[185] https://en.wikipedia.org/wiki/On_Your_Knees_Cave

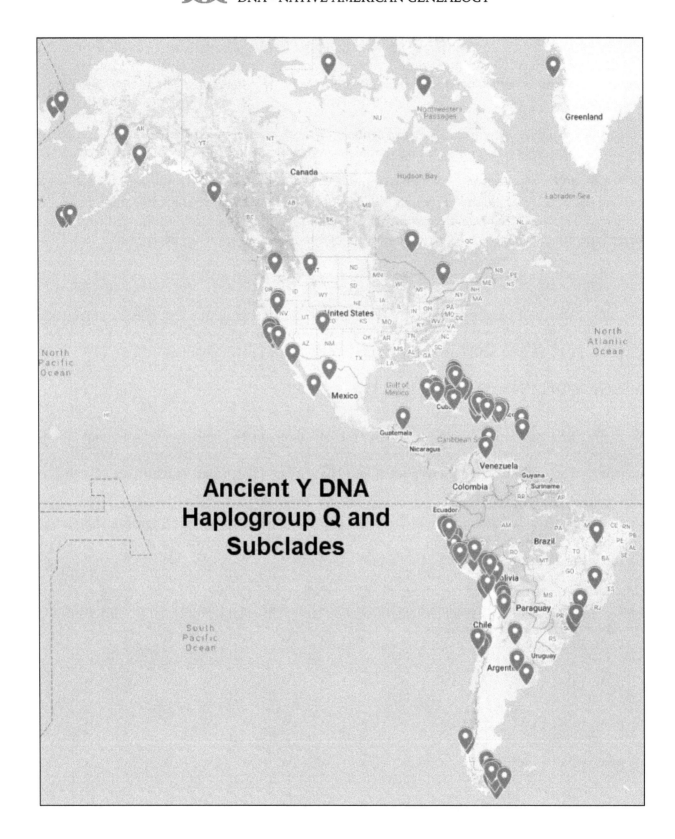

Ancient Y DNA Haplogroup Q and Subclades

The absence of ancient haplogroup Q, as well as C, in the eastern portion of the United States is partly because not many burials have been DNA tested. In addition, fewer burial sites remain since tribes were removed from this area as a result of westward European expansion, and the Native American Graves Protection and Repatriation Act (NAGPRA)[186] complicates testing.

Y DNA Haplogroup Q Tribal Affiliations

Haplogroup Q subclades have been confirmed in the following tribes:

- Achuar
- Apache
- Arasaeri
- Ashaninka
- Awajun
- Aymara
- Ayoreo
- Aztec
- Baniwa
- Bluejacket Shawnee
- Catio
- Chanca
- Chatahuita (Peru)
- Cherokee
- Cheyenne
- Chickasaw
- Chiman
- Chippewa
- Chiquitano
- Chiticano
- Choctaw
- Cocama/Kokama
- Cocamilla
- Comanche
- Creek
- Crow
- Desana
- Ese Ejja
- Guarani
- Guarayo (Bolivia)
- Haida
- Hopi
- Huachipaeri
- Huichol
- Hupda
- Inca

- Inuit
- Iroquois
- Kaingang
- Karanki
- Kayapo (Brazil)
- Kekchi Maya
- Kubeo
- Kuripako
- Laguna Pueblo
- Lakota Sioux
- Machiquenga
- Mahican/Wappinger
- Maidu
- Matsiguenga
- Maxacali (Brazil)
- Mayan
- Mescalero Apache
- Mi'kmaq
- Moche
- Mohawk
- Monkor
- Mosenten
- Nahuatl
- Nambikwara
- Navajo
- Ojibwa
- Okiwinge Pueblo
- Oneida
- Otavalo
- Pasto
- Pehuenche
- Pima
- Piratapuyo
- Plains Cree
- Pocomam
- Pueblo peoples

- Quechua
- Reyesano (nearly extinct)
- Seneca
- Shawnee
- Shipibo
- Siriano
- Swampy Cree
- Tacana
- Tarahumara
- Tarasco
- Tariano
- Tapiete
- Tiwa
- Tlingit
- Toba
- Totonac
- Trinitario
- Tsimane
- Tukano
- Tuyuca
- Uru/Uros
- Uru-Chipaya
- Wampanoag
- Wanano
- Wapashano
- Wappinger
- Warango
- Weenhayek
- Yanesha
- Yaqui
- Yine
- Yupik
- Yuracare
- Xavante (Brazil)

---

[186] https://www.nps.gov/subjects/nagpra/index.htm

Many testers do not specify their tribal affiliation, if known, and others haven't joined publicly displayed projects at FamilyTreeDNA or may not know which tribe their ancestors descended from. The Genographic Project information was indispensable for haplogroup Q analysis. Many Genographic testers did include their tribal affiliation.

Contemporary Y-DNA Native Haplogroup Q

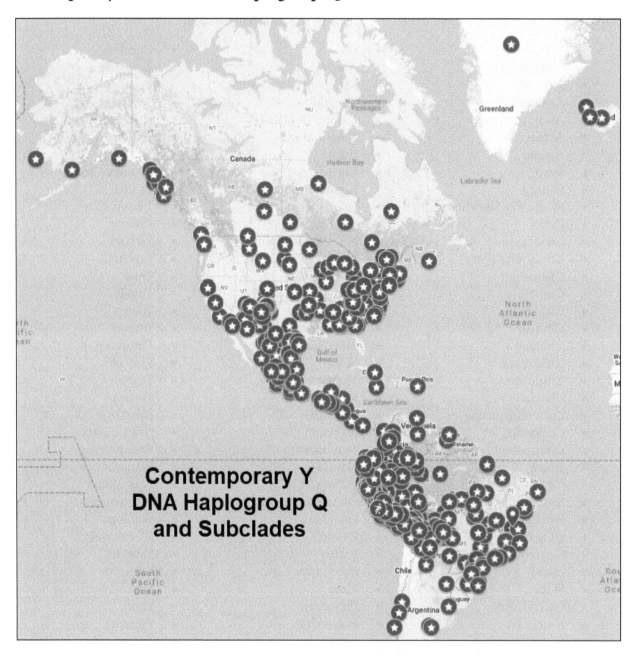

Contemporary Y DNA Haplogroup Q and Subclades

As you can see, haplogroup Q is quite prevalent in indigenous American populations throughout the entire length and breadth of the Americas. Peru and Bolivia have been heavily sampled in academic studies. Other areas, especially in the United States, depend on consumer testing for data.

Haplogroup Q in both Iceland and Greenland is very interesting. The roughly 150 Greenland samples were from Genographic partner academic testing but were only sequenced to the Q-M242 level, which is only base haplogroup Q with no subclade.

All five Icelandic samples are from the Genographic Project. Two early samples were only sequenced to base haplogroup Q1, which includes subclades found in both Europe and the Americas. However, three later samples were sequenced to Q-L804 (the old Q1a1a1a2), which is found most frequently in Scandinavia. This is in keeping with the Viking settlement of Iceland.

Y DNA Native Haplogroup C

Haplogroup C is found throughout Asia and Europe, and it is sparsely scattered in the Americas. It is frequently found in China, Southeast Asia, Oceana, Polynesia, the Pacific Islands, Australia, and New Zealand.

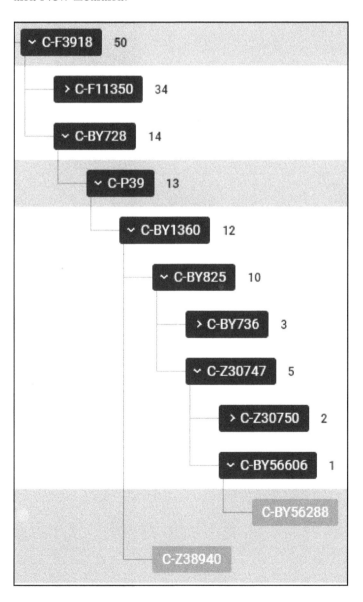

All known Native American haplogroup C falls—besides into haplogroup C itself—into either C-M216; C-M217, the next branch downstream when only high-level testing has been completed; or C-P39 and subclades. One Native tester has been placed in C-F3918, a parent of C-P39, but their testing level is uncertain.

As of September 2021, approximately 110 people show on the FamilyTreeDNA haplotree as indigenous American in haplogroup C, including a few in Mexico, as compared to more than 1,200 people for haplogroup Q.

Ancient Y-DNA Native Haplogroup C

The earliest haplogroup C burial is found in the Ukraine, dating to about 36,000 years ago with a Belgium sample dating to just slightly younger. Other burials, although not as old, are found in Mongolia, Russia, south into Jordan and Israel, and throughout most of Asia and Europe. Haplogroup C is found in the furthest eastern peninsula of Siberia, where people migrated to the Americas when Beringia connected the two land masses.

Ancient Native haplogroup C is very sparsely found in the Americas. Were it not for the one sample found in Lapa do Santo, in Brazil, dating to about 10,000 years ago, and one from the Ecuadorian highlands from 7,000–9,000 years ago, ancient haplogroup C would be entirely absent from South America. Ironically, Lapa do Santo is also the oldest haplogroup C burial.

The Caribbean islands, where two additional haplogroup C samples have been found in Cuba and Puerto Rico, were settled by people who arrived from the South American mainland.

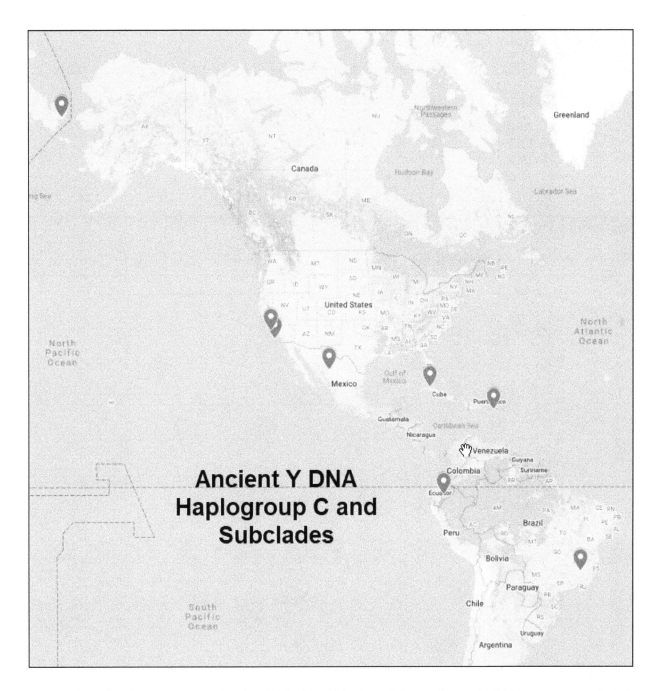

Ancient Y DNA Haplogroup C and Subclades

The earliest haplogroup C Native burial is found in Brazil from about 10,000 years ago, with the earliest US sample located on San Nicolas Island in California from about 2,200 years ago. Haplogroup Q burials are also found on San Nicolas Island beginning about 4,400 years ago.

Bones retrieved from a midden at nearby Point Sal, California, produced haplogroup C and Q samples from about 1,500 years ago.

153

Y DNA Haplogroup C Tribal Affiliations

Haplogroup C is found much less frequently than haplogroup Q in the Native American population.

Haplogroup C subclades have been confirmed in the following tribes:

- Mi'kmaq
- Ojibwa
- Otavalo
- Plains Cree
- Plankishaw
- Quichua
- Seneca
- Tlingit
- Yoruk
- Warango

Contemporary Y DNA Native Haplogroup C

Haplogroup C is found scattered sparsely throughout the Americas.

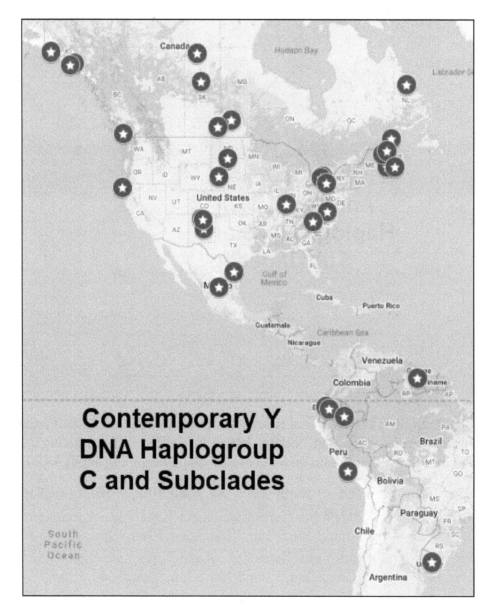

Contemporary Y DNA Haplogroup C and Subclades

While ancient haplogroup C is found in a few burials in the Caribbean, contemporary C has not been found there to date. However, ancient haplogroup C has not been found in Canada or the United States outside of California, but contemporary haplogroup C has been found in both of those regions.

It's possible that haplogroup C was so unusual in some locations that some Y DNA lineages simply died out over time. Another possibility is that so few men have tested from some regions that haplogroup C is out there but is extremely rare, and not yet found in testers.

The Outlier – Y DNA Haplogroups O-FT45548 and O-BY60500

It's probable that a very rare subgroup of haplogroup O is also Native.

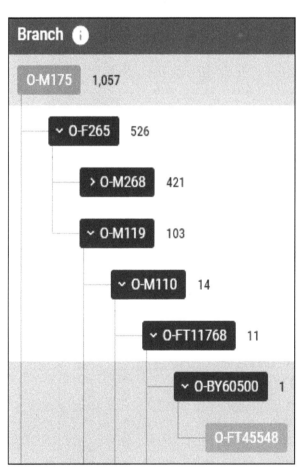

Testers in haplogroup O-BY60500 and subclade O-FT45548 have proven Native American heritage.

We have multiple confirmed men from a common ancestor who is proven to be an enslaved Accomack "Indian boy" named James Revell, born in 1656, "belonging to the Motomkin" village, according to the Accomack County, Virginia, court records. [187] These men tested as members of haplogroup O-F3288 initially, after taking the Big Y-500 test. However, upgrading to the Big Y-700 produced more granular results and branches reflecting mutations that occurred since their progenitor was born in 1656.

Unfortunately, other than known descendants, these men have few close Y DNA or Big Y-700 matches. Without additional men testing from different unrelated lines, or ancient haplogroup O being discovered, we cannot confirm that this haplogroup O male's ancestors were not introduced into the Matomkin Tribe in some way post-contact. Today, one descendant from this line is a member of the Lumbee Tribe.

However, that isn't the end of the haplogroup O story.

---

[187] http://www.familyheritageresearchcommunity.org/delmarva-dna

The Genographic data shows one Haplogroup O Tlingit tribal member from Taku, Alaska, along with several testers from Mexico who indicate their paternal line is indigenous. Some people from Texas identify their paternal line as Hispanic.

Another individual indicates they were born on the Fountain Indian Reserve in British Columbia and spoke St'at'imcets, the language of the interior branch of Coastal Salish.

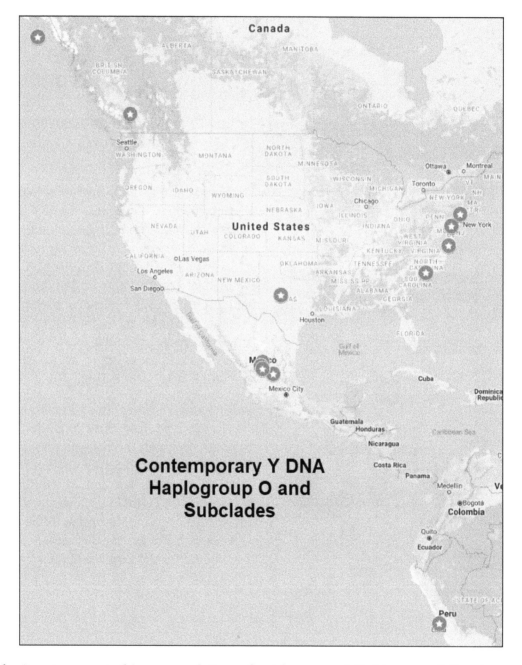

While I don't yet suggest this accumulation of evidence as definitive proof, I'm increasingly convinced that haplogroup O is indeed indigenous, just in vanishingly small quantities and spread very thinly.

It's particularly interesting that we see a small cluster of four individuals in interior Mexico. The FamilyTreeDNA haplotree shows 10 people at the O-M175 level in Mexico; 9 people in the United States report of Native heritage, 2 in Jamaica, 1 in Peru, and 1 in Panama. Altogether, this gives us about 35 haplogroup O males, several with Native heritage.

Finding Y and Mitochondrial DNA Testers

If you're a female or a male who doesn't descend directly from the male ancestor in question, you'll need to find a proxy tester—meaning a male in your family line who does descend from the suspected male Native ancestor through all males and who is willing to take a Y DNA test.

If you want to confirm that an ancestor was Native on their mother's side, you'll need to find someone, male or female, descended from that female ancestor through all females to the current generation.

Autosomal DNA testing spans all your ancestral lines, but for Y and mitochondrial DNA you're looking for people descended in specific ways from your ancestors of interest.

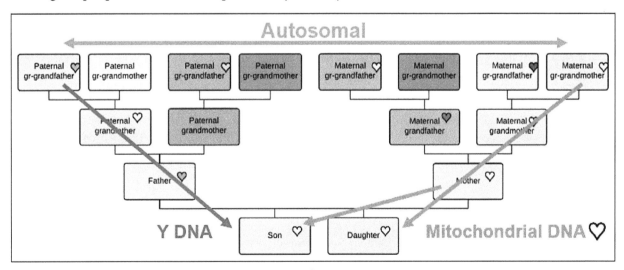

There are several ways to find an appropriate person. The first step is to look at the tree descending from the ancestor in question. Determine if there is someone that you already know who descends appropriately.

With males this tends to be relatively easy, of course. If great-great-grandpa Jones is the suspected Native person, then you're looking for a Jones male today—assuming the surname has stayed intact in subsequent generations. Y DNA in the United States typically follows the male surname line.

Mitochondrial DNA is different because the surname generally changes in every generation when the female marries. You're looking for direct lines of females to the current generation. The current generation tester can be female or male because women give their mitochondrial DNA to both sexes of their children—but only females pass it on.

Search at Ancestry, MyHeritage, FamilyTreeDNA, WikiTree, and other genealogy "family tree" sites for other genealogists who have included the people you are seeking in their trees. Specifically, you're looking for someone who is either a descendant themselves or seems to be closely related to a descendant and is interested in genealogy. Use the tester's email or the vendor's messaging application to establish contact. I generally start out by asking questions and sharing some information.

- Assuming you've DNA tested at Ancestry, use ThruLines[188] to see if you match someone descended from that ancestor who would be a candidate for either Y DNA or mitochondrial testing. Contact that person.

- At MyHeritage, view your Theories of Family Relativity (TOFR)[189] for each of your matches to determine if they descend from that ancestor appropriately. I always make a note on each match as to our common ancestor, so I don't have to view the entire match record each time.

- At FamilyTreeDNA, upload or create a tree, and link everyone who matches you to their proper place in the tree. This allows FamilyTreeDNA to use triangulation[190] to assign people to the proper side of your tree, maternal or paternal, making it easy to see if someone who has already tested has taken the Y or mitochondrial test you need. If not, reach out and ask if they will. I always offer to pay for their test.

- At FamilyTreeDNA, you can also download your entire match list that includes the Y and mitochondrial DNA haplogroups, and earliest-known ancestors for your autosomal matches who have taken those tests, by clicking on "Export CSV" on the Family Finder matches page.[191]

[188] https://dna-explained.com/2020/02/22/optimizing-your-tree-at-ancestry-for-more-hints-dna-thrulines/; https://dna-explained.com/2019/03/11/ancestrys-thrulines-dissected-how-to-use-and-not-get-bit-by-the-gators/
[189] https://dna-explained.com/2020/09/23/myheritage-updates-theories-of-family-relativity-who-is-waiting-for-you/; https://dna-explained.com/2021/02/12/how-can-you-get-theories-of-family-relativity-at-myheritage/
[190] https://dna-explained.com/2019/11/06/triangulation-in-action-at-family-tree-dna/
[191] https://dna-explained.com/2021/03/31/how-to-download-your-dna-matching-segment-data-and-why-you-should/

The matches download also provides other information, including ancestral surnames (if the tester has entered the information), if they are bucketed maternally or paternally, and any notes you've made. This information will assist you in locating someone from the right family and will tell you if they have already tested. If they have tested at least at a high-level haplogroup, you will be able, in some cases, to exclude Native ancestry. In other cases, the test may show a haplogroup that *might* be native, but you'll have to do more testing to get a definitive answer. Of course, you may need to contact them and ask if they would be willing to upgrade their test to a higher level.

Additionally, there may be people from the right family who don't match you, but you can view a list of projects. At FamilyTreeDNA, you can check relevant projects to see if someone who descends from the ancestor you seek has already tested.

Males may have joined surname projects. If you are seeking an Estes male, for example, check the Estes surname project to see if anyone from the line you're interested in has already tested. You can view surname projects by Googling "Estes DNA project at FamilyTreeDNA." You can also go to the main FamilyTreeDNA page and scroll down until you see the Search Surname function.

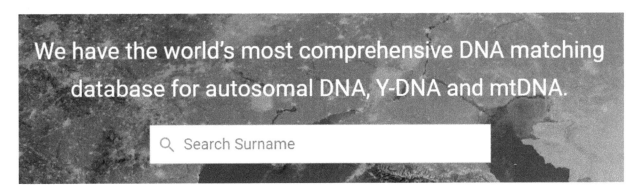

You will be able to see how many people with that surname have tested, including males and females, and any projects that welcome people with that surname.

You can also search on various types of words, such as "Indian" or "Acadian" or any other word that might help you locate people descended from that ancestor.

As mentioned earlier, if I ask someone to take a test, I always offer to pay for it. They aren't testing for themselves—they are testing for me. I make sure to provide them with an explanation of what was discovered and what it means.

At WikiTree,[192] if you search for your ancestor, then click on their profile, it will reveal if any other WikiTree users have taken Y, autosomal, or mitochondrial DNA tests that are relevant for that ancestor. If not, clicking on "Descendants" will show you a list of descendants whom, in some cases, you can trace to the current generation.

---

[192] https://www.wikitree.com/

PART 6

YOUR ROADMAP *and* CHECKLIST

A Roadmap and Checklist for You to Follow

Now that we've discussed the aspects of Native American DNA and associated cultural and genealogical considerations, let's put together a roadmap and checklist for you.

We've discussed most of these items. Hopefully you'll make progress as you work through this list.

Your status should be something relevant to you, such as "yes," "no," or maybe "in the process."

Task	Vendor/Tools	Your Status
Talk to family members and document details about your family stories.		
Check information at traditional genealogy sites for documentation and information about potential Native ancestors.	FamilySearch, MyHeritage, Ancestry, WikiTree, Google searches	
If a potential Native ancestor is in your direct matrilineal line, purchase a full sequence mitochondrial DNA test.	FamilyTreeDNA maternal ancestry mtFull Sequence test	
If you are a male and your potential Native ancestor is in your direct patrilineal line, purchase a Y DNA test.	FamilyTreeDNA paternal ancestry Y-37 will provide a predicted haplogroup. If the predicted haplogroup is Q, C, or O, upgrade to the Big Y test for the most refined haplogroup.	
Order autosomal tests for ethnicity/population results.	Order directly from 23andMe and Ancestry. They do not allow transfers from other vendors.	
Transfer your autosomal DNA results from either Ancestry or 23andMe to FamilyTreeDNA and MyHeritage.	You will need to unlock advanced tools for $19 and $29, respectively, to obtain ethnicity results and access to advanced tools. It's much	

	less expensive than retesting.	
Check your 23andMe Ancestry Composition results and your FamilyTreeDNA myOrigins results to see if you have either Native or Siberian/Russian DNA segments.	If so, download your ethnicity segments at 23andMe and FamilyTreeDNA.	
Upload the 23andMe and FamilyTreeDNA ethnicity file download to DNAPainter.	DNAPainter	
Identify people who match you on your Native segment(s) by comparing your results at 23andMe and FamilyTreeDNA to determine if those individuals have Native DNA and if they match you on your Native segment.	Download your DNA match segment file[193] into a spreadsheet and sort by location and chromosome to determine who matches you on that segment. You will have two groups, maternal and paternal.	
Identify which side of your tree, maternal or paternal, the Native DNA descends from.	View the individuals who match you on that segment, looking for groups of people who also have Native heritage.	
At FamilyTreeDNA, viewing your match list and sorting your segment match file will allow you to separate the people who have been bucketed to your maternal and paternal sides on your Native segment.	FamilyTreeDNA	
Sort your matches into paternal and maternal sides on your Native segment(s).	Download your DNA match segment file[194] into a spreadsheet and sort by location and chromosome to determine who matches you on that segment. You will have two groups, maternal and paternal.	
At FamilyTreeDNA, view Y and mtDNA haplogroups of your matches looking for Native haplogroup candidates.	You can do this by clicking on their profile card or by downloading your match file.	

---

[193] https://dna-explained.com/2021/03/31/how-to-download-your-dna-matching-segment-data-and-why-you-should/
[194] https://dna-explained.com/2021/03/31/how-to-download-your-dna-matching-segment-data-and-why-you-should/

View trees of people who match you on the Native DNA segment, or those who have Native haplogroups, to identify common ancestors.	All vendors except 23andMe, which doesn't support user trees	
Use GeneticAffairs AutoTree[195] feature, which automatically compares the trees of AutoCluster members searching for common ancestors in your and your matches' trees.	GeneticAffairs[196]	
Use GeneticAffairs AutoSegment[197] feature to cluster your matches by segment match, quickly identifying groups of people who match on specific segments.	GeneticAffairs	
Utilize DNAPainter[198] to upload your ethnicity segment data and identify which ancestors contributed your Native segments.[199]	DNAPainter[200]	
Use DNAPainter to identify people who match you on your Native segments[201] to locate potential candidates for Y and mitochondrial DNA testing.	DNAPainter	
Watch the webinar "10 Ways to Find Your Native American Ancestor Using Y, Mitochondrial and Autosomal DNA"	Legacy Family Tree Webinars[202]	
Create a DNA Pedigree Chart	Genealogy tree software	

---

[195] https://geneticaffairs.com/features-autotree.html

[196] https://dna-explained.com/2020/08/13/genetic-affairs-instructions-and-resources/

[197] https://geneticaffairs.com/features-autosegment.html

[198] https://dnapainter.com/

[199] https://dna-explained.com/2019/08/29/native-american-minority-ancestors-identified-using-dnapainter-plus-ethnicity-segments/

[200] https://dna-explained.com/2019/10/14/dnapainter-instructions-and-resources/

[201] https://dna-explained.com/2020/04/01/triangulation-in-action-at-dnapainter/

[202] https://dna-explained.com/2021/09/04/free-webinar-10-ways-to-find-your-native-american-ancestor-using-y-mitochondrial-and-autosomal-dna/

You Don't Know What You Don't Know

You may think you know which ancestor or ancestors contributed your Native American DNA, but what if you've pegged the wrong ancestor, or maybe you have Native ancestors whom you don't know about?

While autosomal DNA divides in half in each generation—eventually creating segments so small that they can't be attributed to a specific ancestor, and then perhaps washing out altogether—Y and mitochondrial DNA never do. It doesn't matter how far back in time your Native American ancestor resides in your tree, their Y and mitochondrial DNA will always be Native, and you can always find it!

Every male ancestor has a Y chromosome and every person in your tree has mitochondrial DNA.

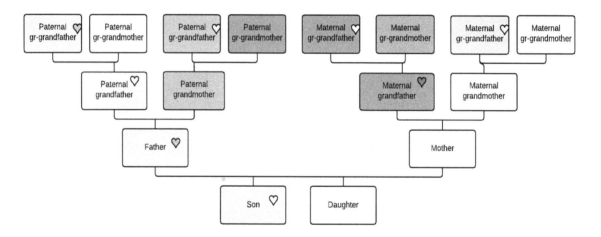

This pedigree chart of your great-grandparents illustrates that you can discover four Y haplogroups and eight mitochondrial DNA haplogroups. People who share your great-grandparents are your second cousins, whom you may well know. Each generation further back in time doubles the potential number of Y and mitochondrial DNA haplogroups that you can collect.

One of my genealogical priorities is to find a tester to represent every family line. That's **exactly** how I identified which of my Acadian ancestors were Native, and which were not. Proving that an ancestor is not maternally or paternally Native is every bit as useful as proving that they are.

Either way, you find matches with the potential to push that line further back in time, and you learn about your ancestor's history through their haplogroup, before written records.

Enjoy the Journey – Follow the Breadcrumbs

I hope you enjoy the search for your ancestors. Discovering information about their lives, genetic or otherwise, helps us understand their journey—and all the journeys of our many ancestors that together became our own.

While all four types of DNA testing and results—ethnicity, autosomal matching, mitochondrial, and Y DNA—are uniquely useful, mitochondrial and Y DNA can reach further back in time.

To break down your brick walls, the best research plan is to utilize all these types of DNA and methodologies, along with all the wonderful tools available.

Try every avenue, and don't forget to check back periodically to see if there are new matches or new clues.

Your ancestors are waiting for you. What can you discover?

GLOSSARY

Admixture

In the genetic genealogy world, admixture refers to the different populations or ethnicities reported by vendors.

Ancestry

Genealogy company that offers both genealogical records for research and AncestryDNA autosomal DNA testing. To fully utilize DNA results—including advanced tools, the ability to view other testers' complete trees, and other benefits—a subscription to their genealogical services is required. Ancestry does not accept uploads from other vendors.[203]

Ancestry Chromosome Painting

At 23andMe, painting the tester's different ethnicity segments on their chromosome pairs.

Ancestry Composition

The ethnicity tool at 23andMe.

Ancestry Timeline

At 23andMe, an estimate of when your ancestor with a specific ethnicity might have lived.

Ancient DNA

DNA retrieved from burials.

AutoCluster

A visualization tool created by GeneticAffairs using cluster technology that groups your matches into colorful clusters based on who matches each other in addition to matching you.

Autosomal DNA

50% of autosomal DNA is inherited from each parent for chromosomes 1–22. The X chromosome is sometimes included in autosomal DNA products and is sometimes referred to separately or not at all due to its unique inheritance path.

Autosomes

Chromosomes 1–22.

Beringia

The land mass that connected Russia with Alaska before Beringia was covered by the sea approximately 11,000 years ago.[204]

---

[203] https://support.ancestry.com/s/article/AncestryDNA-with-an-Ancestry-Subscription-US-1460090085520-3160
[204] https://en.wikipedia.org/wiki/Beringia

BIA

The Bureau of Indian Affairs in the United States.[205]

Big Y

Currently known as the Big Y-700. At FamilyTreeDNA, a test of discovery that sequences the majority of the Y chromosome in order to determine the most refined haplogroup and discover mutations that provide additional family genealogical information. Known as the Big Y test, this was previously known as the Big Y-500.

Biogeographical Ancestry

A term originally coined to represent individuals' various populations components. Today, each vendor calls this component of its autosomal DNA offering something different, but the most common, generic term is "ethnicity."

Blood Quantum

The amount of Native American DNA individuals possess based on their genealogy, generally expressed either as a fraction or a percent. Blood quantum is required to obtain a CDIB card and is often one of the components utilized by tribes in determining eligibility for membership.

CDIB Card

The CDIB (Certificate of Degree of Indian Blood) card, issued by the Bureau of Indian Affairs (BIA). To apply, the degree of blood quantum must be provided, along with other information.

Centimorgan

Written as cM, a centimorgan is a unit of measure on a chromosome. Vendors establish a minimum cM length, as well as a minimum number of SNPs within the segment of DNA that qualifies as a match for autosomal DNA testing.

Chromosome Painting

The third-party tool, DNAPainter, facilitates two types of chromosome painting. Users can paint segments of their chromosomes with matches in order to associate segments of their DNA with specific ancestors, or they can upload their ethnicity results from either 23andMe or FamilyTreeDNA, both of whom provide chromosome painting as part of their autosomal DNA product. Combining the two types of chromosome painting provides the ability to match specific ethnicity segments with an ancestor from whom the segment descended.

Compare Origins

At FamilyTreeDNA, a tool that allows customers to compare their ethnicity with others, and also displays the locations of their matches' Y and mitochondrial DNA ancestors on a map.

---

[205] https://www.bia.gov/

Cultural Appropriation

> The act of a more powerful culture, or a person from a more powerful culture, adopting or claiming a tradition or item from a less powerful culture as their own.

Directional Mating

> A situation in which one population selectively mates with another. In the context of Native Americans and the Spanish, specifically in Mexico, Spanish men participated in directional mating with Native American women because there were few non-Native women available as partners.

DNA

> Deoxyribonucleic acid is a molecule that coils into a helix and provides genetic instructions for reproduction.[206]

DNAPainter

> A third-party application introduced by Jonny Perl that provides a variety of tools, including the ability to paint segments on a canvas of blank chromosomes in order to identify matches with common DNA segments, inferring common ancestors.

DNA Sequencing

> The process in a laboratory that reveals the sequence of nucleotides in DNA.

DNA Testing

> For genealogy, swab or spit tests submitted to testing companies to obtain ethnicity breakdown and autosomal, mitochondrial, and Y DNA matching results with other testers, based on the vendors' product offerings and the test ordered.

DNA Tests

> Genealogical DNA tests are available from four major vendors, who provide an autosomal DNA product, including matching, though each vendor provides some unique features. FamilyTreeDNA also provides Y and mitochondrial DNA testing for genealogy.

Double Helix

> The familiar shape of both strands of the DNA molecule.

Endogamy

> The custom of marrying within a community or clan. In genetic terms, the result is that many of the community members share common DNA segments of distant founder ancestors.

Ethnicity

> Generally speaking, a social group that has a common national or cultural tradition and whose members identify with one another based on shared attributes. In terms of genetic

---

[206] https://en.wikipedia.org/wiki/DNA

genealogy, ethnicity is the breakdown of populations and geographies that can be determined (estimated) through the use of population genetics.

FamilyTreeDNA

Pioneering genealogical DNA testing company that offers Y DNA, mitochondrial DNA, and autosomal DNA testing through their Family Finder product. FamilyTreeDNA's database includes results from people who tested beginning in 2000 and provides the most advanced sequencing and tools for both Y and mitochondrial DNA. FamilyTreeDNA does not require a subscription for full access if you test with them but has a small unlock fee for advanced tools if you upload your DNA from another vendor.

First Nations

In Canada, groups of indigenous people aren't called tribes but are referred to as First Nations. Generally, this designation excludes Métis, who are mixed, and Inuit peoples considered to be circumpolar, arriving at a later date. The terminology is not without discord.

Full Sequence

For mitochondrial DNA, the full sequence refers to testing all 16,569 locations of the mitochondria, as compared to testing smaller portions. Early tests only tested about 500–1,000 positions for comparison. Today, some vendors who don't test mitochondrial DNA separately test a few locations in order to provide customers with an estimated high-level haplogroup that is included with an autosomal test.

Genealogical Proof Standard (GPS)

The genealogy proof standard was created as a form of guidance provided to genealogists to ensure thorough, accurate research and reasonable conclusions drawn from as much information as possible.[207]

Genetic Affairs

Also written as GeneticAffairs. A company founded by Evert-Jan Blom that provides clustering technology where customers can view clusters of matches that match each other in addition to the tester. Clusters indicate common ancestry between cluster members.

Genetic Communities

At Ancestry, Genetic Communities are locations where individuals whose DNA matches suggest ancestors in common with other testers.

Genetic Genealogy

The application of genetic tools to genealogy. Genetic genealogy has the ability to confirm ancestors, reveal ancestors and relationships, and refute both relationships and

---

[207] https://www.familysearch.org/wiki/en/Genealogical_Proof_Standard; https://bcgcertification.org/ethics-standards/; https://www.familysearch.org/wiki/en/The_Genealogical_Proof_Standard_(National_Institute)

genealogy, including close relationships. Genetic genealogy results must be interpreted accurately and are sometimes inconclusive.

Genetic Groups

At MyHeritage, Genetic Groups are locations where individuals whose DNA matches suggest ancestors in common with other testers.

Genetic Sequence

A number of adjacent DNA locations that are used for comparison to other testers in genealogy. Identical ranges of specifically selected locations that match are genealogically relevant. Mutations are used in both mitochondrial and Y DNA to determine haplogroups.

Genetic Tree

23andMe constructs an estimated genetic tree for you based on your matches from its DNA Relatives feature. Genetic Affairs also provides this functionality, in addition to AutoClusters, with its AutoKinship feature.

Genographic Project

The Genographic Project[208] was launched by the National Geographic Society in April of 2005 with the goal of testing consumers to map the migration of humans across the planet. Customers learned interesting information about their DNA, including Y and mitochondrial DNA base haplogroups, along with some ethnicity information. Sales were discontinued in mid-2019, with the public database being closed at the end of 2020. The DNA and demographic data for participants who selected to participate in research were transferred to the University of Pennsylvania to provide research access after the public portion of the Genographic Project ended. More than one million people from around the world tested with the Genographic Project.

Haplogroup

For Y and mitochondrial DNA, a group of people who share specific mutations that place them in a common genetic clan. Haplogroups, based on a series of mutations, can be traced forward and backward in time.

IBC[209]

Identical by Chance matches occur when autosomal DNA contributed by the mother and father just happens to align in such a way that the segment of DNA matches another individual. However, the match is not a valid genealogical match because it did not descend from an ancestor of either the mother or the father but was a result of random recombination.

---

[208] https://en.wikipedia.org/wiki/Genographic_Project
[209] https://dna-explained.com/2016/03/10/concepts-identical-bydescent-state-population-and-chance/

IBD

Identical by Descent matches occur when the DNA between two individuals matches because they share a common ancestor, and their DNA descends from that ancestor through their parent.

IBS

Identical by State matches occur when individuals are identical by descent, but the segments are small, generally under the matching thresholds of the vendors, and are a 3result of being members of a common population. IBS segments are used in the assignment of ethnicity by mapping DNA segments to populations.

Imputation

A scientific methodology designed to statistically estimate the DNA that would logically be found adjacent to known DNA locations in order to fill in untested regions in situations where DNA raw data files are somewhat incompatible with each other, or are incomplete. Incompatibility occurs when chip versions change, and between different vendors DNA tests.

Indigenous

The original inhabitants of a place. The exact definition and how the word is used varies depending on the circumstances. In terms of Native American people, regardless of their tribal or political affiliation, indigenous people are those originally occupying the Americas prior to European contact or colonialization.

Inheritance

In genetic terms, DNA that people inherit from their parents. Everyone inherits exactly half of each parent's autosomal DNA on chromosomes 1–22. For females the X chromosome, number 23, is inherited in exactly the same way as the autosomes, but males only inherit an X chromosome from their mother. Males inherit a Y chromosome from their father instead of an X, which is what determines their sex. Males and females both inherit mitochondrial DNA from their mothers, but only females pass it on.

Markers

Generally referred to in Y DNA, meaning the STR (Short Tandem Repeat) markers used for genealogical matching. STR markers are reported in test panels of 12, 25, 37, 67, and 111 markers. The Big Y-700 test provides a minimum of 700 STR markers, including the 111 sold in the STR panel tests.

Matching

Vendors compare the DNA of their customers and report matches. It's up to the customer to interpret the match for genealogical relevance.

Match Threshold

Y and mitochondrial DNA matches are determined by genetic distance, meaning how many single location mutations' difference two individuals can have and still be considered a match. An autosomal match threshold is defined by a minimum number of matching centimorgans combined with a minimum number of SNPs. Vendors have different match threshold minimum numbers, and match thresholds change from time to time.

Maternal Side

Your mother's side of the tree, which is not to be confused with a direct matrilineal line. Some vendors refer to mitochondrial DNA as your "maternal" DNA. Unfortunately, this leads some people to misunderstand the mitochondrial DNA pathway and which ancestors contributed their mitochondrial DNA to descendants.

Matrilineal

A matrilineal line is your mother's mother's mother's direct line up your tree through all females. This is the lineage of the mitochondrial DNA.

Mitochondrial DNA

DNA necessary in humans to produce energy. However, genealogically speaking, mitochondrial DNA is a valuable tool for understanding our direct matrilineal line, both historically and in terms of genealogical matching.[210]

Mutation

A change at a DNA location that can (autosomal DNA) or will (Y and mitochondrial DNA) be passed to future generations.

MyHeritage

A genealogy company that offers both genealogical records for research and MyHeritageDNA autosomal DNA testing. Some tools and features are only available with a premium subscription plan.[211] MyHeritage does accept uploads from other vendors and charges a small unlock fee for access to advanced tools.

MyOrigins

The ethnicity or population tool at FamilyTreeDNA.

MyOrigins Chromosome Painting

FamilyTreeDNA's chromosome painting based on populations.

MyOrigins Match Sharing

At FamilyTreeDNA, the ability to view the ethnicity results and Y and mitochondrial DNA locations of matches who opt in for the sharing feature.

NAGPRA

The Native American Graves Repatriation Act sets forth guidelines for repatriating objects, including remains, held by entities—such as governments, museums, and universities—outside the jurisdiction of associated tribes. It also encourages dialogue to

---

[210] https://en.wikipedia.org/wiki/Mitochondrial_DNA
[211] https://www.myheritage.com/pricing

increase understanding and prevent future abuses. NAGPRA requires the agreement of culturally associated tribes before DNA testing can be performed on Native remains.[212]

Nucleotides

Thymine, adenine, guanine, and cytosine—abbreviated as T, A, G, and C — are the building blocks of DNA. Mutations occur when one is substituted for another at a particular genetic location, or a deletion or insertion occurs.

Pairwise Bonding

Occurs when your mother's DNA bonds to the same location in your father's DNA to create the bond between helix strands on each chromosome. Each parent donates one combined copy of each of their chromosomes to a child.

Parental or Trio Phasing

When an autosomal DNA match occurs between two individuals, comparing the matches' DNA to both parents verifies that the DNA descended from one parent and was not randomly combined between both parents to assemble in the child in a way that appears as a match to another human. The process of verifying matches against parents' DNA is known as parental or trio phasing, as compared to statistical or academic phasing, which does not utilize the parents' DNA. Parental phasing is the most accurate way to assign specific nucleotides to either the maternal or paternal copy of the chromosome.

Paternal Side

The father's side of the tree, which is not to be confused with a direct patrilineal line. Some vendors refer to Y DNA as your "paternal" DNA. Unfortunately, this leads some people to misunderstand the Y DNA pathway and which ancestors contributed their Y DNA to descendants.

Patrilineal

Your patrilineal line is your father's father's father's direct line on up the tree. In males the patrilineal line is the source of the Y DNA chromosome, and in western cultures, generally the source of the male's surname as well. Therefore, DNA Y chromosome matching and interpretation are often simplified because the most meaningful matches are often those with the same surnames.

Phasing

Two types of phasing are used in genetic genealogy, parental phasing and academic/statistical phasing.

PhyloTree[213]

A publicly available resource that includes more than 5,400 mitochondrial haplogroups, their defining mutations, and links to the NCBI (National Center for Biotechnology

---

[212] https://www.nps.gov/subjects/nagpra/index.htm; https://www.nps.gov/archeology/tools/laws/nagpra.htm
[213] http://www.phylotree.org/

Information)[214] data uploads of associated mitochondrial sequences utilized in haplogroup definition.

Population Genetics

A specialized field of genetics that focuses on the composition of populations, their relationships to each other, changes within and interchange between populations, and their distribution around the world.

Populations

Related inhabitants of a country or region. In relationship to genetic genealogy, testers are interested in information that connects them with their ancestors' historical populations.

Race

Race is often focused on physical constructs and similarities based on shared ancestry. The constructs of race and ethnicity are often blurred and confusing.

Reference Populations

Populations against which testers are compared for relevance. Generally, each testing company uses a combination of public sources and their own internal database to define the reference populations against which they compare their customers for ethnicity predictions.

SNP

A Single Nucleotide Polymorphism is a single mutation. The abbreviation SNP is commonly pronounced as "snip."

Statistical Phasing

Also called academic phasing to differentiate between statistical phasing and parental or trio phasing. Statistical phasing is a technique using probability to statistically assign DNA segments to specific "sides" of a chromosome based on their neighboring DNA when the parents' DNA is not available for reference. This technique phases or reassembles each chromosome separately, and the parental sides may not be consistently in the same position (top or bottom) on all chromosomes and may occasionally produce switch errors on the same chromosome.

STR

Short Tandem Repeat markers are repeat markers used to compare Y DNA results for genealogical connections.

Strands

The two strands of DNA pictured in the double helix represent the maternal side and the paternal side of the chromosome.

---

[214] https://www.ncbi.nlm.nih.gov/

Treaties

Legal documents that describe agreements between entities—in this case, between governmental units and sovereign tribes. In the United States, the government has a long history of either violating or breaking treaties with tribes.[215]

Triangulation

A genetic genealogy technique in which multiple people (at least three) are proven to match each other on the same reasonably sized segment, confirming that the segment is identical by descent and that the group of matching people share a common ancestor.

Tribal Membership Requirements

Membership requirements are individual to each tribe.

Tribes

Tribes are legal entities and sovereign nations, governing themselves, within the United States.

23andMe

Autosomal DNA testing company that began DNA testing for ancestry in 2007. 23andMe focuses on health and provides both genealogy and health/traits testing, either together or separately. The number of matches is limited, but up to 5,000 matches can be viewed with a membership subscription. 23andMe does not accept uploads from other vendors and is the only vendor that does not support family trees.[216]

X DNA

The X chromosome has a unique inheritance pattern, eliminating some ancestors as the source, which makes chromosome matches on the X chromosome useful to genealogists.[217] The X chromosome is tested as part of autosomal testing but is not reported by some vendors. Of the four major vendors, FamilyTreeDNA and 23andMe both utilize and report X chromosome matching.

Y DNA

The Y chromosome is only inherited by males and is widely used for matching to other males to determine genealogical lineage. STR markers are used in conjunction with SNP data to refine matching to its highest level and provide the most granular haplogroup possible.

---

[215] https://www.archives.gov/research/native-americans/treaties
[216] https://www.23andme.com/membership
[217] https://dna-explained.com/2018/02/07/who-tests-the-x-chromosome/

Printed in the USA
CPSIA information can be obtained
at www.ICGtesting.com
JSHW052328241023
50759JS00018B/315